Style at Home

PRESENTS

MONEY-SAVING
Makeovers

WELCOME

Looking to create your dream home without it costing the earth? In this brand-new bookazine from the makers of Style at Home magazine, we share some of our best tips, tricks, advice and inspiration to help you update your house for less. From DIY hacks and decor ideas to must-have high street finds, your home will feel uniquely you!

Over the following pages, explore the most inspirational home renovations from the most recent issues of Style at Home, including the stunning California-style 1980s bungalow on page 6, as well as the beautiful period townhouse made for socialising on page 44. We've also revealed our favourite garden revamps to inspire you in time for summer!

Elsewhere, discover the best budget-friendly kitchen, bathroom and living room makeovers, featuring on-trend paints, wallpapers, furniture and more, plus storage solutions and fast fixes to help you get the perfect look for your home without breaking the bank.

Contents

STATEMENT
LIGHTS
Page 6

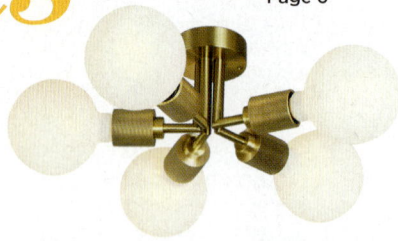

DREAMY
DECOR
Page 122

16

102

116

GENTLE
TONES
Page 106

'It's budget but

A CHIC ENTRANCE
'Hallways can often be overlooked, but I wanted this space to feel consistent with the rest of the house'

CEILING SOLUTION
'We fitted faux beams to hide old light fittings, and also to add character and a natural element in the living and dining areas'

COME ON IN!

ABOUT ME I'm Michaela Shoebridge, a content creator (you can find me at @mishkashoe) and I live here with my partner Lee, who works in sales and marketing, along with our four cats, Frank, Christian, Bella and Eddie.

MY HOME A four-bed bungalow built in the 1980s, in East Yorkshire. We bought it in 2019.

WHEN WE MOVED IN It had bags of potential but needed updating – the majority of the house had been decorated top-to-toe in magnolia and was just bland and lacking character.

AND NOW It's fresh, bright and airy with a high-end design finish that has been achieved on a very limited budget.

STYLE TIP Open shelving throughout a home creates interesting focal points and a chance to display favourite wares.

looks HIGH END'

IDEA TO STEAL

`Faux beams add character and bring a rustic aesthetic to a plain space'

Michaela and Lee have modernised their dated 1980s bungalow, to create a relaxed, Californian style home in the heart of Yorkshire

A s first-time buyers we were keen to find a project we could develop over time, ideally in a quiet, rural location,' says Michaela. 'We'd been renting locally for two years, keeping a keen eye on properties that were coming onto the market – and this four-bedroom bungalow in East Riding, Yorkshire, was perfect.

We loved that the rooms were well proportioned and logically laid out on one level. It had a generous footprint, large back garden and bags of potential to extend and add value.

Changing style

The property had been built in the 1980s and although it needed updating, it wasn't in bad condition. The majority of the house had been decorated top to toe in magnolia and was bland and lacking character. In stark contrast was the jazzy red kitchen, which I'm sure would have been the height of fashion in the early 1990s, but really was a sight to behold!

All the rooms lead from an L-shaped hallway. One side opens into the living, dining and conservatory areas, which has a partial wall and central fireplace to create a divide between them. The kitchen and utility room are accessed from the dining area. On the other side are the bedrooms, study and family bathroom.

Unfortunately, we had a big set-back while we were waiting for the sale to go through – the North had a severe cold snap and the water tank froze, causing the pipes to burst and flood the entire house. There was a lot of water damage which had to be addressed before we could think about anything else, and this ate up a scary amount of our »

LIGHT SPACE
'The dark window frames create a striking contrast against the linen curtains and softer shades used throughout the room'

IDEA TO STEAL
'A double-sided log burner heats both rooms simultaneously'

'WE'VE UNIFIED THESE TWO ROOMS AND LOVE ENTERTAINING IN THIS OPEN-PLAN SPACE NOW – THE UPDATES HAVE CREATED A LITTLE SOCIAL HUB'

OPEN PLAN
'Wood beams and limewashed bricks bring the two areas together'

ON SHOW
'Open shelves in the alcoves are ideal for displaying favourite pieces of art'

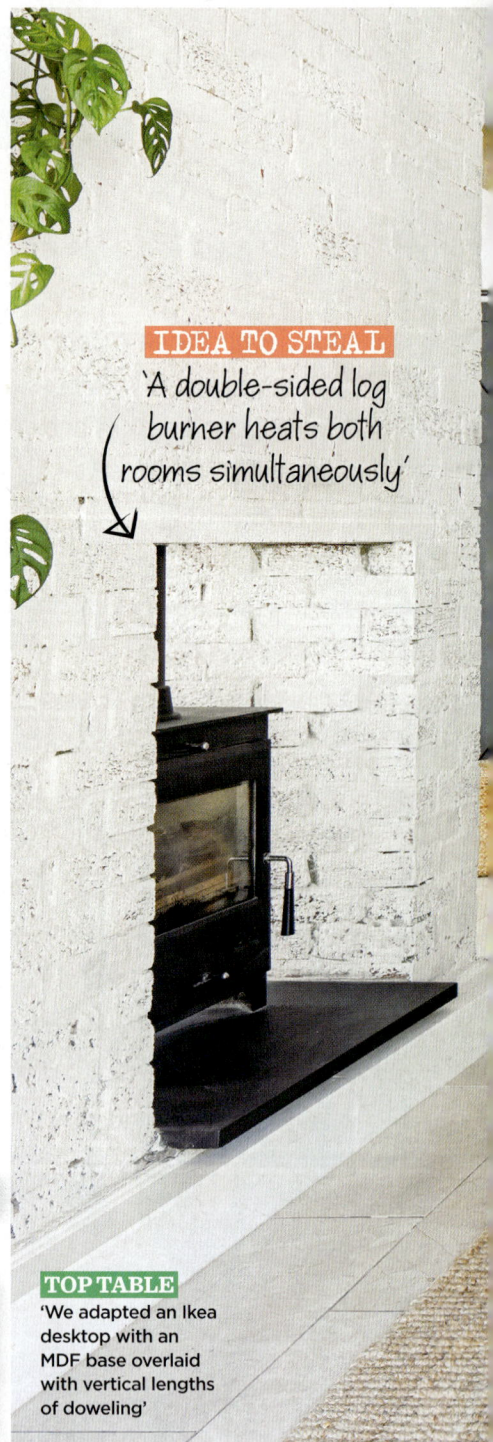

TOP TABLE
'We adapted an Ikea desktop with an MDF base overlaid with vertical lengths of doweling'

›› renovation budget before we had even had a chance to move in!

Forging ahead

Our priority was to remove the old water tank and replace it with a new combi boiler, which was relocated to the utility room. The main bathroom was refitted, with extra space created by the removal of the water tank, allowing for a shower and a small bath. We also removed an ugly old fireplace to reveal

3 of the best STATEMENT LIGHTS
Cast a gorgeous glow with a stunning light fitting

the brickwork, installing a double-sided log burner that serves both the living room and dining area.

The kitchen and utility room have also been given a full makeover, with the existing cupboard doors and worktops professionally wrapped with vinyl from Cover Styl. Floor-to-ceiling cabinets have been built in an unused area and an integrated fridge-freezer added.

We were conscious of not over-spending in this area, as we have plans »

ANTIQUE APPEAL
Industville sleek flat pendant light, Naken

IN LINE
Spiral 6 light bar pendant, Dar Lighting

ALL AROUND
Hoxton ceiling light, Dowsing & Reynolds

CALM AND AIRY
'Internal doors into the conservatory were removed, making it an inviting space to relax'

IDEA TO STEAL
'Low-hanging pendants direct light to exactly where you need it the most'

GO NATURAL
'The red brick walls were plastered and a shelving area built to use as a log store'

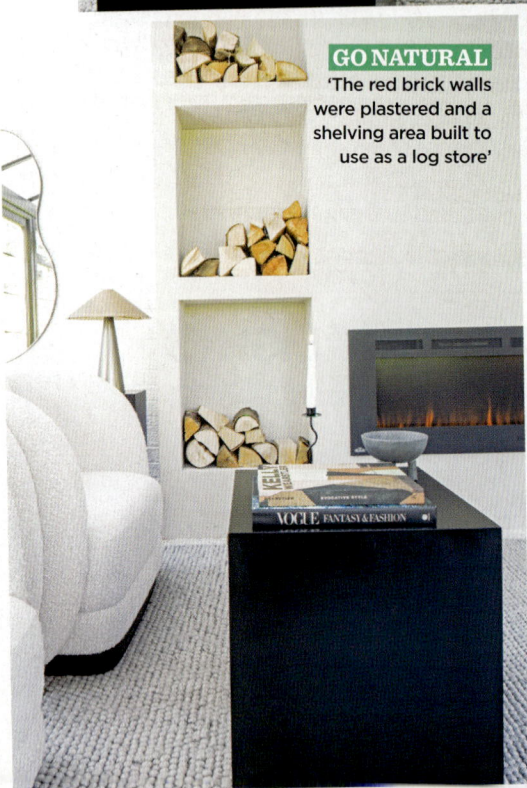

COLOUR SWAP
'With plans to extend in the future, we are very happy with our budget updates... and that the kitchen is no longer red!'

Do it! USE VINYL WRAP

Take inspiration from Michaela's kitchen makeover and modernise existing units with vinyl wrapping.

✳ Vinyl wrapping is the process of applying a sheet of coloured or textured PVC vinyl to a surface to change its look and feel. It's a sustainable, cost-effective way of updating cabinets and worktops without replacing them entirely.

✳ The vinyl sheets come in different sizes and are applied using a combination of heat and specialist tools, which shape the vinyl to the surface it is being fitted on.

✳ The benefits are that it's robust, lasting up to 10 years, and can be up to 80% cheaper than replacing your kitchen. There is a huge range of vinyls to choose from, from faux wood and marble to glitter and soft touch. It is also quick to install, taking an expert around 1-2 days.

✳ It costs around £1,500-£2,000 but cheaper alternatives can be found if you choose to do the work yourself.

'REPURPOSING OUR EXISTING KITCHEN WITH VINYL WRAP HAS BEEN A COMPLETE GAME CHANGER – I CAN'T BELIEVE IT'S THE SAME KITCHEN'

»» to extend and move the kitchen at some point in the future. Lights have been replaced, radiators covered, and internal doors replaced with sliding ones. Each room has been replastered and decorated, and barn doors and ceiling beams added to the living areas.

Overcoming challenges

Aside from the flood before we'd even got the keys, our biggest issue has been working with a very limited budget. This was squeezed even further with the onset of the pandemic, which had a huge negative impact on our income and really pushed up the cost of labour and materials. We were forced to reassess our plans for the house and become more creative with ideas, swapping structural changes for more achievable aesthetic alterations.

We also realised we could drastically cut costs by taking on much of the work ourselves, obsessively researching what was required for each stage, and watching hours of DIY tutorials »»

UTILITY UPDATE
'The utility room keeps laundry appliances out of sight and is home to the new boiler'

TILE STYLE
'The patterned floor tiles and wall tiles in a herringbone design look great together'

BATHING SPACE
'A small reconfiguration has given us enough room for a shower and a small bath. It works perfectly for us'

online. Every step of the way we have gained new skills, and despite the steep learning curve, our confidence has grown, and our plans have become bigger and more ambitious.

New roles

At the beginning of the renovation, we started an Instagram account – @mishkashoe – to document our journey and use as a forum to share ideas. Fast-forward three years and our account has blossomed and I have taken on a full-time role as an interiors content creator – it's opened so many new doors! For complete novices, not

'I love the simplicity of Scandi design. The pared-back birch furniture from Ikea and linen-dressed bed makes you feel instantly calm'

IDEA TO STEAL

'Convert a handy nook in the wardrobe into desk space'

TUCKED AWAY

'We added panelling and a shelf here for extra storage'

'YOU CAN MAKE CHANGES WITHOUT SPENDING A LOT – IT'S OK TO UPCYCLE AND MAKE SOMETHING WORK UNTIL YOU CAN AFFORD THE REAL DEAL'

Do it... CREATE A RELAXING ENVIRONMENT

✳ When your home is cluttered and chaotic it's difficult to feel relaxed, so start by decluttering.

✳ Decorate in muted, neutral tones which are easy on the eye and promote the calmest, sanctuary-like vibes.

✳ Use plenty of texture for interest – soft fabrics create a cosy feel, while natural materials offer a more rustic finish.

✳ Ensure you have a variety of lighting types, from natural, ambient and task lighting, in each room. That way your space will feel more inviting.

✳ Work in scent – from candles and essential oil diffusers to flowers, getting a fragrance that instantly helps you relax is key.

STATEMENT PIECE
'I designed and fitted a bespoke headboard along the length of the wall to add a touch of comfort and luxury'

IDEA TO STEAL
'A neat ledge finishes off the headboard and doubles up for display'

SUBTLE DEPTH
'The walls have been painted in a soft grey, lime-based chalk paint'

FEATURE MARISHA TAYLOR/LAURIE DAVIDSON
PHOTOGRAPHS JAMES FRENCH

Where to buy Michaela's style

✳ **LA REDOUTE** Buy homeware, furniture and fashion at reasonable prices. Always worth looking out for their seasonal sales.

✳ **IKEA** Classic Swedish style that is ideal if you want a clean, simplistic look.

✳ **GREEN LILI** Modern wall art for cosy spaces, like the large abstract design in Michaela's living room. From framed prints to large canvas art, there's something for every scheme, whatever its size and style.

✳ **HM HOME** For on-trend interior pieces, such as the two low rattan armchairs Michaela has in the living room. HM Home is known for its affordable prices and it's good to keep your eyes peeled as new items launch all the time.

✳ **DUNELM** Great for rugs, such as the large grey pebble rug in Michaela's conservatory, as well as all other homeware. Again, Dunelm's prices won't break the bank.

>> knowing much about renovations and learning along the way, we have created a home full of warmth and character that makes us very proud. I wanted the decor to be smart but make the space feel calm and relaxing, and we've achieved this by using a soft colour palette, natural elements and modern design touches. We've really thought about how to mix rustic, natural and modern elements in an understated and uncluttered way – I think the house now has a real sense of calm and continuity, and a unique, high-end look which hasn't broken the bank. It's better than we could have ever envisaged.'

'OUR HOME IS FRESH, BRIGHT AND AIRY WITH A HIGH-END DESIGN FINISH THAT HAS ALL BEEN ACHIEVED ON A VERY LIMITED BUDGET'

RAW FINISH
'Internal doors have been replaced with wooden sliding ones'

SUNNY SEATING
'The neutral colour scheme, punctuated with black accents, continues into the garden'

'I like to mix up

COME ON IN!

ABOUT ME I'm Temi Johnson, a criminal defence lawyer and an interior designer (for my design services go to temijohnson.com; @ahousemadeofbrass). I live here with my husband Benoit, an actor and teacher, and our son Phoenix.

MY HOME A two-bed end-of-terrace in Stanstead Abbotts, Hertfordshire, built in 1890 by the great great grandfather of one of our neighbours! We moved here in December 2018.

WHEN WE MOVED IN The bones of the house were good, but it needed modernising and replastering.

AND NOW It's beautifully colourful, with a new kitchen and laundry room.

STYLE TIP Have fun with it. Part of the joy for me is to scour car-boot sales to get those unique pieces.

OLD AND NEW'

UPCYCLED STYLE
'Our Ercol sofa and brass coffee table came from eBay and I've added my favourite artwork – my mum gave me the lady wearing the fez, so that is special to me'

Temi Johnson has decorated her beautiful home with unique finds and a vibrant colour palette that lifts the spirits all year round

Designing my home was a life-changing move for me,' says Temi. 'It cemented my decision to pursue a career in interior design full time and led to me appearing on TV's *Interior Design Masters* this year.

'It was love at first sight when we spotted this house and we were thrilled it came in within our budget. At the time, I was living with my husband on a narrow boat while we saved for our mortgage, which is funny as when I first met Benoit I remember being distinctly unimpressed by the fact he lived on a boat and saying I wouldn't be joining him. Fast forward a few years and I'd not only moved onto the boat, but also found that I really enjoyed living on the water. It was that time that actually led to us buying our house in this village, as we used to take the boat into the Hertfordshire countryside in the summer and always said that when we bought a house, it would be here. In fact, in a funny turn of events, we somehow ended up living right next door to the boat yard we used to take the boat to for repairs!

Instant attraction
This house has good links to London, yet you feel like you're in the middle of the countryside with the nature reserve, canals and the river all on your doorstep. It wasn't only the location though – I knew I wanted a house with two double bedrooms, which this place has, plus we'll probably consider a loft conversion at some point and the second bedroom is large enough that it can potentially lose some space to a staircase if needed.

Challenges ahead
It wasn't going to be easy sailing, however, as the house needed a lot »

IDEA TO STEAL
Furniture on legs will help a small footprint seem bigger'

UNIQUE PIECES
'The old radio is another piece I inherited from my mother. She wasn't even using it; I think it had been in the shed. The lamp was a present from Benoit's mum'

'I GREW UP IN A HOUSE FULL OF ANTIQUES AND VINTAGE FINDS — YOU CAN'T BEAT THE CHARACTER AND CHARM OF SOMETHING OLD'

3 of the best VIBRANT COLOURS
Paint boring walls with a mood-lifting pop of colour

GOLDEN TOUCH
Gamboge pure flat emulsion, Paint & Paper Library

SKY BRIGHT
Passionate Lilac matt paint, YesColours

FIERY HUE
Bamboozle modern emulsion, Farrow & Ball

BRIGHT ADDITIONS
'When we moved in the shutters were already in place. I bought the Ercol chairs from eBay. They're my best bargain buy'

of work doing to it. Every room needed modernising and redecorating – the bathroom even had the old soil pipe visible, which oddly we didn't notice when we viewed the house. That said, the original parquet flooring was still intact and the previous owners had installed a small kitchen extension, so at least we had enough space for a nice kitchen area.

We completely ripped out the downstairs kitchen and old shower room, turning the space into a kitchen and laundry room instead, with a downstairs loo. This was supposed to take around six weeks, but due to building issues the whole thing took nearly three months – that's a long time to be washing up in the bath tub! I knew I wanted a decent-size kitchen as I love to entertain and for me, food is life. Up until recently when we redecorated our bedroom, I would have said the kitchen was my favourite room as it's the heart of the house and where we spend most of our time when we have friends or family over. It's such a nice space to entertain in while I'm cooking. Our dining table was left by the previous owners, and they'd made it from an old boat, which felt really fitting seeing as we lived on one before moving in here. I don't think I'd fully realised the state

IDEA TO STEAL

'In the summer, use your fireplace as a spot for plants'

HAPPY HOUR
'The guitar belongs to my husband – it tends to come out after he's made one of his famous cocktails!'

>> that the place was in, as pieces of furniture had been covering some holes in the walls when we'd viewed it. Safe to say, it was a bit more than the cosmetic makeover I had been hoping for! Despite that, we got stuck in, ripping up all the carpets, sanding the floorboards and painting each room.

Adding colour

Because these houses are tiny, our aim was to use colour and furniture to make the space feel bigger and more inviting, and I think we've achieved this, especially in the living room. I chose paint for all the walls as I have an irrational dislike of >>

'YOU CAN'T BEAT THE CHARACTER AND CHARM OF SOMETHING OLD'

HIDDEN STORAGE
'The pantry is probably my favourite thing other than the island. It's a literal godsend and hides everything'

FARMHOUSE FEEL
'I wanted a traditional country-style kitchen, so I chose a butler's sink, while the taps and cabinetry handles are all in brass'

IDEA TO STEAL
'Use lighting in the
same finish to keep
your style consistent'

DREAM KITCHEN
'The cream Esse cooker
was kept from the existing
kitchen. The units are
from Olive & Barr. I knew I
wanted a green kitchen –
a shade that could feel
traditional but also fun'

OUT OF SIGHT
'The laundry room is a life saver, especially as the washing machine and dryer are neatly hidden away'

Do it... SHOP SECONDHAND

✳ If you're shopping for a piece of furniture or larger item, make sure you've taken accurate measurements beforehand. You'll need to measure not only the space it's going to fit in, but also any doors or entrances that it will need to pass through. Take a tape measure with you while shopping, so you can ensure your chosen piece will fit.

✳ Once you've found your preloved item, check it thoroughly. Often, vintage pieces won't be immaculate and that's all part of the charm, but you don't want to get home to find that drawers or doors don't open, or that it has woodworm.

✳ When it comes to car-boot sales, be prepared to haggle. If you're picking up a few pieces, why not ask the seller for a deal as you're buying more than one?

✳ Think about how you can transform pieces – maybe it's not in the right colour for your scheme, or you don't like the handles, but these are all factors you could easily change.

'DON'T RUSH WHEN IT COMES TO DECORATING – TAKE TIME TO FIND ITEMS YOU REALLY LOVE'

➤➤ wallpaper! The bright orange paint in here is an eco-friendly limewash from Francesca's Paints. She hand-mixes all her paints in her studio in Clapham, and I went to visit her to choose the colour.

Upstairs changes
The bathroom was a bit of a hidden surprise for us as not only had we not noticed the hole in the bottom wall or the exposed soil pipe when we first looked around the house, but the room had also been modified for disability. Strangely, someone had put a plastic sheet across the wall above the bathtub and drilled a hand rail onto it, so there weren't any tiles or anything of that nature.

We didn't change the layout, but I bought a bath and sink secondhand on eBay, and then swapped out all the plumbing so it was all fresh. I'd definitely change a couple of the details in here, mainly to do with the quality of one or two of the fittings, but I can always upgrade them later down the line.

Unique style
Putting our stamp on the place was the best bit, and I think the majority of the items in our house are secondhand. I ➤➤

SNUG SPOT
'Investing in a raised bed from Ikea allows us to store all of Phoenix's toys underneath, as well as giving him space to play'

'The tepee was a gift from Phoenix's godmum – he uses it as a little snug area or as a spot for hide and seek'

IDEA TO STEAL

'Make tidy-up time fun by storing toys or clothes in a cute basket'

IDEA TO STEAL
'Bring the outside in by growing a plant around the headboard or posts'

Do it! USE BOLD COLOURS

✳ You don't have to have large rooms to use bold colours. Instead, ramp up the cosy feel with rich, dark colours or go for all-out drama with fun, vibrant shades.

✳ Paint walls and woodwork the same colour to help maximise the space from walls to ceiling, creating the illusion of height.

✳ If you're not brave enough to paint your walls in a bold colour, why not try a standout piece of furniture instead, such as a dining table, island unit or a bookcase?

✳ Choose a colour with warmer tones for a north-facing room, where the light is colder, whereas south-facing rooms are ideal for darker, richer shades.

'I FIND PINTEREST INSPIRING WHEN I HAVE AN IDEA IN MY HEAD AND WANT TO SEE IF ANYONE ELSE HAS DONE IT AND WHAT IT LOOKED LIKE'

❯❯ love antiques and vintage finds and in my opinion, you can't beat the character and charm of something old. I like to mix in the old with a bit of modern, so I think my style is a combination of traditional meets modern vintage with a shed-load of colour thrown in! Not only will buying secondhand save you money, but it's better for the environment and things were often made much better "back in the day", so you won't compromise on quality. I started to do a weekly car-boot story on my Instagram page before winter came because I was there every weekend without fail. I'm obsessed! There's a lot left to do, and so much snagging to fix which definitely gives me a twitchy eye whenever I see it, but for the budget we had I can't complain and I'm pleased with how the house has turned out and what we've achieved so far.'

Find more clever ideas to style up your home by going to **Instagram / @styleathomemag**

FEATURE LAURIE DAVIDSON PHOTOGRAPHS LIZZIE ORME

PASTEL SCHEME
'Our bed is a birch bed from Ikea and I was shocked by how good the quality was. The walls are painted in Dulux's Bright Skies, while the door colour is matched to Farrow & Ball's Arsenic'

Where to buy Temi's style

✳ **THE EDITION 94** A treasure trove boutique filled with beautiful pieces from makers and artisans, along with vintage homeware.

✳ **HOMEPLACE** An eclectic mix of vintage, mid-century, retro and contemporary furniture, lighting, accessories and homeware.

✳ **HUTCH COMMUNITY** An online community, full of inspiration. You can buy, sell and browse secondhand interiors and furniture.

✳ **MAYFLY VINTAGE** Find original vintage furniture, lighting and homeware, with everything from industrial to French style.

✳ **ETSY** An online marketplace where you can purchase unique items from across the globe, with a focus on handmade or vintage pieces.

HANDLE IT
'I had the wardrobe built to fit an alcove in the bedroom and asked for curved door inserts for interest'

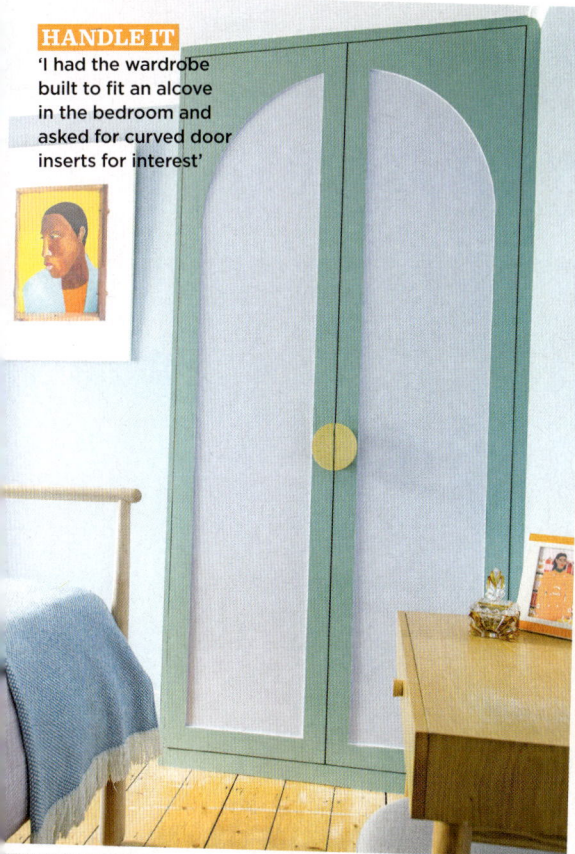

NEUTRAL CHOICE
'The bathroom is small and I knew I wanted a design that wasn't typical for a small space. The brass really stands out with a neutral colour scheme'

SMART SCHEME
'By adding new doors by Howdens, an island unit and new tiles, we transformed the original standard kitchen. The stools are from Dunelm'

DARK & INTERESTING
'Gold handles finish the look. The print is from Print Club London'

COME ON IN!

ABOUT ME I'm Elise Dodds (@makemynewbuildpretty), and I work in HR. I live here with my husband Michael, a management consultant, and our two children Elodie and Huxley.

OUR HOME Four-bed detached new build in Whitley Bay, Tyne & Wear.

WHEN WE MOVED IN We bought the house in March 2016, and slowly started to do work on it.

AND NOW We converted the garage to a playroom, knocked through the utility room and fitted sliding doors. We also re-tiled the bathrooms.

STYLE TIP I like to change the feel of our rooms for the seasons using different textiles and cushions.

is full of COLOUR'

IDEA TO STEAL

'Add lights under wall cabinets for extra illumination'

When Elise Dodds started adding colour to her new-build home, there was no stopping her

With our first baby on the way, we felt it was time to leave our small rented flat in north London and buy a more affordable property near our families,' says Elise. 'Our flat in Islington was open plan and we didn't even have an internal door we could close!

Although my husband Michael and I had met in London, our families only lived a mile away from each other in the North East, so it was the perfect time to move back to be near them.

We'd both lived in period properties before and loved their character, but I was drawn to a more modern and practical type of property. This led us to buy a new-build house off-plan on a Taylor Wimpey estate in Whitley Bay. We loved the old terraces in nearby Tynemouth, but they weren't great for a young family. They lacked parking and we didn't think we'd have time for a renovation. Buying a new build was just so much easier.

Moving in
Six weeks before our daughter Elodie was born, we moved into the house, which had basic fittings from the developer's limited options. I became pregnant again six months later with son Huxley, and we were thankful not to have a big renovation project on the go.

When the children started to walk, our priority was to convert the garage into a playroom and also to landscape the garden with raised beds and lots of grasses to draw the eye away from the walls and fence. It was quite an investment at the time, but it's been so worthwhile as the garden really feels like an extension of our home.

Next steps
Two years later we decided to knock through our corridor-like utility room to create a bigger dining area with four-metre wide bifold doors replacing ➤

'Use dark colours on just half a wall for a more subtle look'

COASTIE

GALLERY WALL
'The Opening Hours picture is actually a framed tea towel. The beanbag is from Icon'

'I WANTED TO PROVE THAT NEW BUILDS CAN HAVE THEIR OWN PERSONALITY AND CHARACTER'

» the double patio doors. We'd spent all that money on the garden but couldn't really see it, so choosing a design with narrow frames and as much glass as possible has worked out really well.

To make up for losing the utility room, we installed floor-to-ceiling kitchen cabinets in the dining area, which conceal our washing machine and dryer, alongside additional storage. At the same time, we gave the white gloss kitchen an overhaul. It felt criminal to pull something out that had only been in five years, so we just replaced the base unit doors, added an island and changed the handles, lighting, sink, tap and worktops.

Long wait

With family life taking precedence, decorating was on the back burner and we always felt like it was a temporary home – it stayed in its basic white state for nearly five years! One day I said to Michael, "I can't live with it like this anymore". It wasn't joyful to come home as it didn't feel cosy or reflect our personalities. Having read a tip about »

BRIGHT BUY
'The yellow Ikea sofa stands out perfectly against walls in Farrow & Ball's Hague Blue. I bought the coffee table in New York'

Oh I do like to be beside the seaside

LIGHT UP
'The neon light will come with us from house to house as I can't imagine not living by the sea now'

3 of the best TYPOGRAPHIC ART
Make a statement with a vibrant display

YOU ARE MAGIC

SPELL BINDING
All Seeing Eye poster, Grace Digital Art Co

THIS KITCHEN IS FOR DANCING

DISCO MOVES
This Kitchen Is For Dancing print, Hidden Prints

KINDNESS

GET THE MESSAGE
Kindness art print, Fy!

taking cues from your clothes, I opened my wardrobe door to reveal an array of pinks, greens, yellows, blues and lots of prints – my wardrobe was full of colour but my house wasn't!

All change

I was determined to add personality to our home and smash the stereotype of the new-build white box – I wanted to prove that they can also have their own personality and character. With both of us

working from home during lockdown, we started by painting our bedroom walls green. It made such a difference and felt much warmer. Before long, I was experimenting with wallpaper and adding neon lights, as well as painting the staircase and internal doors off-black, replacing radiators with traditional-style designs and investing in shutters. The bathroom and en suite were also given a new lease of life with new tiles and showers, while each of the four »

DREAMY SCHEME
'Elodie really wanted rainbows when we re-decorated her bedroom, and this wallpaper from Eleanor Bowmer is perfect'

IDEA TO STEAL
'Use a dinner plate as a template to create a painted scallop border'

Do it PAINT A SCALLOPED BORDER

Add personality to your room by painting the walls with a scalloped-edge border. Paint them with the scallops facing up or down, on a half wall, a three-quarter wall, or even around the ceiling.

1 Start by using a spirit level and pencil to draw a line across your wall where you want your scallops to sit. Next, take a circular object (plates are ideal) and mark the halfway point on your plate using a piece of masking tape.

2 Line up your plate, with the taped halfway mark sitting on your pencil line, and carefully draw around the top of the plate to create your first scallop. Repeat this all the way along.

3 Paint the scallops and the rest of the wall, leave to dry, then repeat with a second coat.

'MY WARDROBE WAS FULL OF PINK, BLUE, GREEN, YELLOW AND LOTS OF PRINTS BUT MY HOUSE WASN'T!'

COLOUR COMBO
'I fell in love with green and pink Mandarin Stone tiles for the family bathroom'

IDEA TO STEAL

'Use a vertical shelf to stack books in the same colour'

> 'YOU HAVE TO TAKE IT SLOWLY AND LIVE IN THE HOUSE FOR A WHILE, OTHERWISE YOU'LL MAKE MISTAKES BY BUYING THINGS TOO QUICKLY'

›› bedrooms now has its own identity. You can revamp bedrooms so easily by buying different textiles and cushions. I like to change the feel of the room for the seasons, too.

The living room was one of the last spaces to be transformed. It had too much furniture in it, including a large grey sofa that made the room feel really small, so I replaced it with a neater yellow velvet design. By that time, I felt there was a thread running through the house and

knew what colours would work. I loved Farrow & Ball's Hague Blue and this was the ideal place to use it. Because it's not a huge room, I just painted the bottom two-thirds and it immediately felt cosier.

Worth the wait

I'm glad I took my time with the transformation. You have to take it slowly and live in the house for a while, otherwise you'll make mistakes by buying things too quickly. I've loved making the

best of what we've got and adding unique touches that reflect us as a family and where we live, while taking into account the practicality of having small children. As much as we love our home now, neither of us have lost our passion for period properties, so next it'll be a case of waiting for the right house that we can turn into our forever home.'

Find more clever ideas to style up your home by going to Instagram / @styleathomemag

GREEN PARTY

'We painted this room in Tropical Oasis by Benjamin Moore. The colourful bedding is from Kip & Co and the vertical book shelf is by Tee Books'

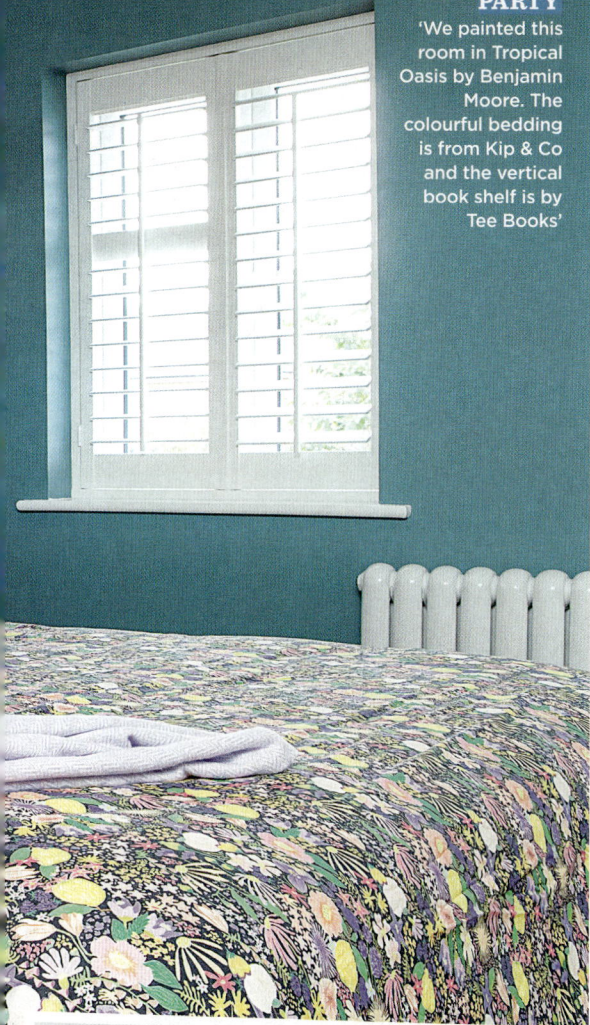

GOING DOTTY

'The dot stickers from Bobby Rabbit made it easy to decorate Huxley's bedroom'

IN BLACK & WHITE

'Tiles from Mandarin Stone plus a smart new shower unit gave our en suite a chic makeover'

Where to buy Elise's style

✳ **FY!** Browse online for a wide choice of colourful artwork, from typographical posters to bohemian-style prints.

✳ **HOMESENSE** A great store for those one-off, eclectic treasures.

✳ **LUST HOME** Quirky and unique wallpapers that make a real statement, plus gorgeous

eco-conscious paint all designed by the in-house team.

✳ **BRILLIANT NEON** This company specialises in custom-made LED neon signs and lights in a variety of colours.

✳ **ANTHROPOLOGIE** Beautiful home accessories, from bedlinen to cushions and throws.

WORDS KAREN WILSON AND LAURIE DAVIDSON PHOTOGRAPHS KATIE LEE

IN HARMONY
'I love finding ways to bring colour and pattern together'

COME ON IN!

ABOUT ME I'm Mary Kilvert, an illustrator, designer and shop owner (marykilvert.com), and I live here with my husband Simon, a procurement director, and our children, Milly, Leo and Rose.

MY HOME A three-bed terraced period house in Frome, Somerset, which we bought in 2014.

WHEN WE MOVED IN The house was only a two bed and quite dated, with woodchip wallpaper, old carpets and ceilings that needed replacing.

AND NOW We opened up the kitchen to the garden, converted the loft and decorated throughout to make it lovely and light.

STYLE TIP It's good to live in your home for a bit before making big decisions about what you want to do with it.

'Every room has

INTO THE BLUE
'We painted the walls in Farrow & Ball's Inchyra Blue – it's my favourite room. Instead of getting a new sofa, I got our existing one reupholstered so it would fit in with our colour scheme'

A PATTERN POP'

IDEA TO STEAL

'Hang unusual decorations for interest'

Illustrator Mary's terraced home in Somerset provides the perfect canvas for many of her colourful designs

Ten years ago my husband Simon and I decided to up sticks and move from south-west London,' says Mary. 'We wanted to find a base for the business and a new home – and as soon as we visited Frome in Somerset we knew it was where we wanted to be based. It's an independent market town with lots going on, surrounded by beautiful countryside.

On the day we visited, I saw the For Sale sign in the window of a shop at the top of Catherine Hill and I knew I wanted it to be my shop. We knew Frome would make a great place to have a young family and so the next step was finding a house. We were after somewhere with period features, a garden and that was close to town – luckily we didn't have to search for long, and found a place pretty quickly.

Finding the one

Built around 1902, this house was originally a two-bedroom property, which the previous owner had lived in for 25 years. Although it had been looked after, it was dated, with woodchip wallpaper, old carpets and plaster on the walls. Despite that, we could see its potential and knew we'd be able to convert the loft further down the line – it was perfect for us.

Once we got the keys, we didn't move in straight away. We replastered the whole house, and replaced carpets in some rooms and sanded floorboards in others. It took around two months, but it was worth it and we finally moved in two months before our first child was born.

Major work begins

Changing the layout slightly was something we were keen to do, as the house had a kitchen with an old boiler and utility room, which blocked access »

IDEA TO STEAL
'Have bespoke shelving made specially to fit an awkward space'

FEATURE WALL
'The fireplace works with the period of the property and creates a focal point for the room – I spent a year finding tiles that feel sympathetic to the house and add interest'

3 of the best...
FLORAL WALLPAPERS
Roll out a design that brings your wall into full bloom

DELICATE DESIGN
Miss Daisy
wallpaper, I Love
Wallpaper

WILD AT HEART
She's a Wildflower wallpaper
in Brights on Vintage
Cream, Lust Home

FOLKSY FEEL
Alice Green
wallpaper, Victory
Colours

'THE KITCHEN IS NOW A NICE LIGHT SPACE AND THE
EXTENSION HELPS CONNECT THE OUTDOORS WITH IT'

>> to the outside space. We got the builders in and created an extension to remove the utility room and turn the space into a kitchen-diner that leads out to the garden. We went for a modern, simple feel with handleless cupboards and a mint-coloured Smeg fridge-freezer which was a bargain from eBay. We then found a carpenter to build cupboards under our stairs, which has been useful for extra storage – they're wallpapered with a colourful design from Borastapeter.

It's such a nice light space now and the extension has helped connect the outdoors with it. Our patio area feels like an extra room and it's a great place to sit with family and friends during the summer months.

Moving up
Next up was the loft conversion, which took around two months to complete, but was essential to create some much-needed space for us due >>

BRIGHT SPOT
'We inherited our Ercol dining chairs from family and then bought some other chairs secondhand, which we painted'

IDEA TO STEAL

'Make a galley kitchen feel wider by opting for open shelving instead of upper units'

NEW ADDITION

'We chose handleless cupboards for a modern look and had quartz worktops made by a local company'

'I MIX MODERN, CONTEMPORARY STYLE WITH PERIOD FEATURES TO BRING TOGETHER A UNIQUE MIX OF COLOUR AND PATTERN'

to our growing family. I use the loft room as a studio and it's a lovely calm space to retreat to. This room was probably the biggest challenge because we had a little toddler and another baby on the way, so we moved out of the house while the work was being done.

Setting the tone

I like modern, contemporary style with period features and was keen to bring this, together with a mix of colour and

pattern, to our home. I take ideas from interiors magazines, books, and even museums, cafes, exhibitions or places on holiday – and Simon's parents have always had homes filled with beautiful things, which I've found inspiring. I also think it's good not to be afraid of colour as it can be transformative.

When I'm choosing colours, instead of painting little squares on the walls I like to paint big boards and carry them around the house – it's a great way of seeing how a colour can work within a room and how the light affects it at different times of the day. In the living room I went bold, painting the walls in

Quick-fire confession

Your biggest regret?

'We ended up having to redo the floor in the kitchen as we chose the wrong stain. However, it was worth re-sanding and re-staining it to get the finish we wanted'

Do it! ARRANGE DISPLAY PLATES

✳ Mary has used decorative plates on the shelves in her kitchen. To do similar, either install a safety groove along your shelf to help prevent plates from slipping off, or invest in some plate holders to keep them upright.

✳ Style up a collection of plates together in a shape such as a triangle or circle.

✳ Paint the backdrop to your plates in a bold colour to really make them stand out.

✳ Mix sizes, colourways and patterns for a look that's unique to your home style.

PRETTY PRINTS
'I sell lots of kitchenware in my online shop'

CHEERY BACKDROP
'My best buy was the encaustic tiles that we used for the splashback – they're from Claybrook Studio and I love the colour and pattern'

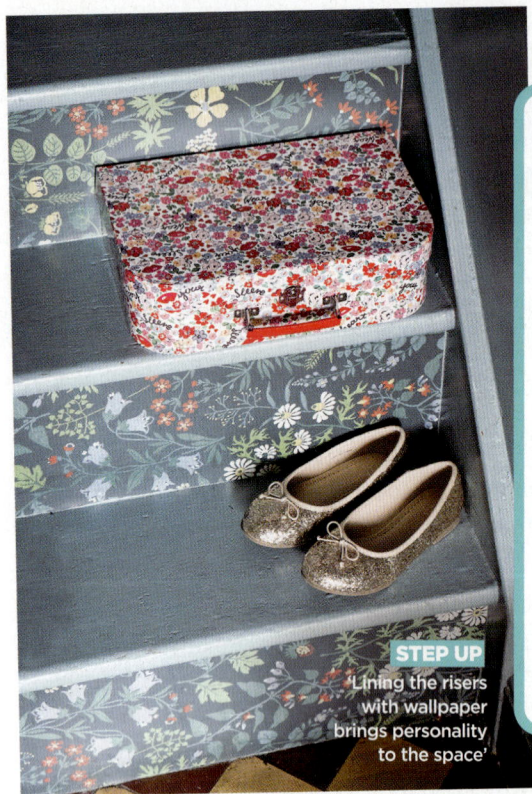

STEP UP
'Lining the risers with wallpaper brings personality to the space'

Do it!
WALLPAPER STAIR RISERS

1 First, prep and sand the stairs – this will make it easier for the wallpaper to adhere to the steps.

2 Measure the riser vertically and horizontally, before cutting a piece of wallpaper to fit.

3 Apply wallpaper paste to the riser, before pressing the paper into position. Use a spatula to smooth out any air bubbles, working from the centre outwards.

4 Once dry, add a coat of varnish to help avoid scuff marks and keep it looking good for longer.

5 Keep an extra roll of your chosen wallpaper handy, for any future touch-ups.

Farrow & Ball's Inchyra Blue. It's my favourite room and a great place to cosy up with a book and hot chocolate in the evenings. We removed the fire in this room soon after we moved in because it wasn't original to the house and didn't look in keeping. Instead, I found our current fireplace at a reclamation yard and got a carpenter to fix the surround for me. Then it took me a year to find the tiles I wanted to use! I finally found hand-painted ones by William De Morgan – I love the colour of them and how they work with the living room scheme.

Designs on display

As an illustrator, many of the designs I'm working on are featured around our home, like prints, textiles and ceramics, and our children are always drawing and making things, so their creations are often on display as well.

Items from my shop sometimes end up in our home, too, and I love collecting textiles, ornaments and paintings and seeing how they come together

'I TAKE IDEAS FROM EVERYWHERE... MAGAZINES, MUSEUMS, CAFES, EXHIBITIONS – EVEN PLACES WE VISIT ON HOLIDAY'

MINT CONDITION
'The tiles are from Mandarin Stone – we love how they work with the colour of the floor'

FLOAT AWAY
'We sell the hanging hot air balloons in our shop'

GET CRAFTY

'Converting the loft meant I gained a studio and it's a lovely calm space to work in. My office chair is from Ikea'

ANIMAL MAGIC

'I get a lot of inspiration for my designs from nature'

NEAT NICHE

'I love displaying one-off pieces from antiques shops and flea markets'

>> to bring personality to a space. I like to use nature and animals as inspiration when I'm designing and these often feature in our home.

Finished result

The last room to tackle was to give the bathroom a fresh new look, and this was completed during lockdown. As soon as it was finished, it felt like the whole house came together. Our next job is to pay some attention to the garden. We're so pleased with how our home has worked out – it reflects us as a family and we've put new life back into it.'

FEATURE LAURIE DAVIDSON **PHOTOGRAPHS** COLIN POOLE

PERFECTLY PRETTY
'We painted the wall behind the bed in Teresa's Green, and the floor paint is Oval Room Blue by Farrow & Ball'

RESTFUL SPOT
'The chair in the bedroom is from a Scandinavian company, and I got the wall hanging online'

'I LIKE THE CALMING FEEL WE'VE CREATED IN OUR BEDROOM – WE CHOSE A SOFT COLOUR PALETTE, PAINTING THE WALL IN A SOOTHING GREEN'

Where to buy Mary's style

WELLS RECLAMATION An eclectic reclamation yard that's set over five and a half acres – it's one of the largest sources of architectural antiques and salvage in the country.

MARYKILVERT.COM From interior accessories to kitchenware, wallpaper and stationery, Mary designs and stocks a range of beautiful products, including her signature woollen sheep.

ANTHROPOLOGIE Unexpected, distinctive finds, including unique furniture and homeware.

BAILEYS HOME A mix of time-worn antiques, textiles and objects alongside contemporary furniture.

'This is a house of TWO HALVES'

While the front of Leila's home features dark, moody chill-out spaces, the rear is light and bright and made for socialising

W e viewed a few properties before this house, all within a mile radius of Grimsby town centre, but we ended up falling for the cheapest and most dated house of all,' says Leila. 'Having rented on and off for years – and having got travelling out of our systems – Joe and I were ready to buy our first home. We lived on the rural outskirts before, so we wanted to be more central.

I'd always loved my aunt's deceptively spacious London terrace and Joe had grown up in a period home, too, so we were on the same page in our hunt for a characterful house. Luckily the three bedroom house we found already had central heating and a new roof, and we couldn't wait to make our own mark on it.

Work begins

On the day we moved in, Joe's Nana was ripping up the worn carpets in the dining room. And the first weekend I started with an easy job by painting the small downstairs toilet. Then we decorated our bedroom in a pale stone grey and painted the floorboards white to create a sanctuary from all the building work we had planned.

By viewing other similar properties, we'd got a feel for what could be done, so a few months later we had the dining room, tiny kitchen and utility room knocked through to create one long kitchen-diner. The ceiling was vaulted and skylights added, while a window and side door were blocked up to give more scope for placing kitchen units and furniture.

Helping hand

After contacting lots of trades people – and only half of them providing estimates! – we eventually found a builder recommended by one of my best friends. However, we had a few challenges during the four-month project. A damp proof course was an unexpected cost and Joe had to fit the bifold doors with his dad because the builder wasn't comfortable installing an unfamiliar product that I'd sourced.

Thankfully the new space, with its galley kitchen in the middle, flows so much better. We regularly have family over for Sunday tea and we love games nights with friends. It's great being able to prep in the kitchen while chatting and we can shift the table and have late-night kitchen discos.

Shortly afterwards, we got the same team to knock the front living room through to the dining room, with Joe »

COSY CORNER 'Joe wanted to go dark right up to the coving. I'm so pleased we did in the end, as it feels really cocooning'

TREASURED PIECES

'I love this room. We got the rug in here from eBay and the sofa came from our previous home'

IDEA TO STEAL

'The white lamp set against the dark curtain and wall colour makes a striking contrast'

Quick-fire confession

What's your best bargain?

'The 1950s coffee table was £70 from a vintage fair in Liverpool. When we got home we googled it and discovered it's a designer piece that can sell for £350 to £450!

SNUGGLE UP
'This Snuggler sofa from Snug was ideal for here as it's small enough to be angled in this corner but we can both sit on it'

'WE LOVE PERIOD FEATURES AND WANTED TO RESTORE AS MANY AS WE COULD TO THIS HOUSE, WHILE MAKING IT FEEL MODERN'

3 of the best DARK PAINTS

Gorgeous colours that suit this statement style

VIVA ESPAÑA
Spanish Brown absolute matt emulsion, Little Greene

MOODY BLUE
Deep Navy Blue ultimate multi-surface paint, Next

DEEP PURPLE
Mallow pure matt emulsion, Fenwick & Tilbrook

≫ (he's a structural engineer) working out calculations for a new steel beam. Previously, the room had a dado rail with red and magnolia walls, but this was removed before the walls were replastered and the floorboards sanded. We also restored a bay window, which was jammed due to years of layer upon layer of paint.

Choosing a scheme

Over the years, I think we've honed our bold interiors style, combining a mix of contemporary and traditional. We love period features and wanted to restore as many as we could to this house, while also making it feel modern. The living room and bedroom at the front are just for me and Joe to relax in, so we went ≫

IDEA TO STEAL

'Tile the riser part of a step to create added interest'

SIMPLY SLEEK

'We chose handleless high-gloss units from Wren Kitchens as the wipeable surfaces are easy to look after. We also wanted wood worktops. They are higher maintenance but we sand and reseal them every year'

IDEA TO STEAL

'Paint a wall mural to tie in the colours you have around your home'

LET'S DANCE

FUN ZONE
'I painted the mural four years ago and added the neon sign (from Neon Beach) for a nightclub feel. The pendant lights are from Swoon'

'I ALWAYS WANTED PARQUET FLOORING AND CONSIDERED RECLAIMED BUT IT WOULD'VE BEEN A MASSIVE TASK, SO WE WENT FOR LVT INSTEAD'

DELICIOUSLY DARK
'When we saw the original tiled flooring, that was the clincher. The painted staircase and black Anaglypta really sets it off'

for dark, cosy colours, whereas the back of the house was kept bright, colourful and fun for when we have friends and family around. We love making an impact, and I very much enjoy telling family and friends my decor ideas and waiting for their reactions!

Now the only pieces of furniture we have from our previous property are a brown leather sofa in the living room and a Peacock chair in the main bedroom. Most of our furniture is ►►

CHOOSING COLOURS
'I painted one wall and the ceiling in green to add some character, with an accent wallpaper opposite. The wallpaper is from Lust Home while the chest of drawers is vintage'

Do it! PAINT A WALL MURAL

Follow Leila's example and be bold enough to create your own artwork on a wall in your home

1 Prepare your wall by making sure it's free of dust or dirt, and repair any scratches or holes.

2 Apply your first coat of paint to the wall and leave to dry.

3 Mark out your design with a pencil so you know which areas you're painting. Then apply masking tape to the pencil lines.

4 Using a paint roller or brush, fill in your first shapes using your chosen colour, being careful not to go outside the edges of the tape. Allow to dry before painting a second coat.

5 Once dry, remove the masking tape from your first shapes, and reapply new strips of tape to mark off the next shapes, repeating the process in step 4.

6 Finally, take the tape off to reveal your finished design.

WHAT A FIND!
'The fireplace and hearth tiles were a fab discovery. They had been boarded up and covered with carpet'

'Use gold leaf to create your own mural – stunning against a dark paint colour'

BOLD DESIGN
'After three years living with pale grey walls, the success of our dark living room encouraged us to go dark in our bedroom, too, and we painted it in Forever and Ever by Coat Paints. We love it'

'WE CALL OUR BEDROOM THE WOMB ROOM AS IT'S SO COCOONING AND RELAXING. WE'VE KEPT THE AREA ABOVE THE BED PLAIN, SO THE DRAMATIC ALCOVES ARE THE FOCUS'

Where to buy Leila's style

✴ **IKEA** It's the go-to place for Swedish-style furniture and accessories, such as Leila's dining table, chairs and record player stand.

✴ **SWOON** for distinctive home decor, with plenty of statement pieces of furniture.

✴ **CROWN PAINTS** Leila painted the stairs in Rebel, which is available in a tough and washable finish – ideal for heavy-use areas.

✴ **EBAY** A great source of low-cost and one-off finds – from rugs and chairs to lights and cushions.

✴ **ABIGAIL AHERN** Find curated pieces that transcend trends, including textiles, lighting, furniture, accessories and paint colours.

IN THE PINK
'The wall colour (Hearts Afire from Valspar) was a bit of a wild card, but it works really well with the black hardware'

'After taking an Abigail Ahern interiors course, I felt more able to curate a display. She suggests grouping items at different heights in sets of three. I chose artwork with flecks of gold to tie in with the murals'

Do it! USE DARK HUES

Here's how to embrace the dark interiors trend

✳ Start by choosing your paint type wisely. If you're worried it could make your room too dark, choose gloss, which has the highest shine, while matt emulsion is good for rooms where the walls could get marked as it will help to hide any fingerprints.

✳ Paint your skirting boards and radiators in the same dark colour, to help blend them in and ensure the wall looks taller.

✳ In a small room try painting the colour up to a picture rail and above it in the same colour as the ceiling, so the ceiling colour 'folds down' – and helps the room appear bigger.

✳ Lift the dark colour with an accent shade – a zingy yellow or a metallic.

ITEMS OF INTEREST

'The vintage brass lamp base just had a bare bulb for some time – until I found this lovely shade from Emma J Shipley'

secondhand and I'll typically look on various home websites first, but then always try and find the same thing secondhand or cheaper on eBay.

Favourite spaces

While Joe loves the living room, where he had the most creative input, my favourite room is the hallway, with its daring black paintwork, fun striped runner and original floor tiles. It just feels so true to our style and the period of the house. It's an instant wow factor every time we come in, and shows our character straight away.

Luckily, we have never disagreed on anything and share a similar vision. Colour drenching the bedroom from ceiling to floor was Joe's idea. If anything,

he's a tiny bit more daring, which encourages me. Next, I'd like to change the layout of our bedroom so the bed faces the window, which would reveal the original hearth tiles currently covered by the bed. It would be lovely to re-instate a fireplace, but we'd need to move a radiator to flip the bed onto the internal wall, so that's a job for the future.

Looking ahead

We've updated the garden recently and now we can't imagine moving for a very long time. We've put our absolute hearts into this home. It's our fifth year here and I don't think I could bring myself to sell it as there's been too much blood, sweat and tears. We've created our dream home and I'd be gutted to leave.'

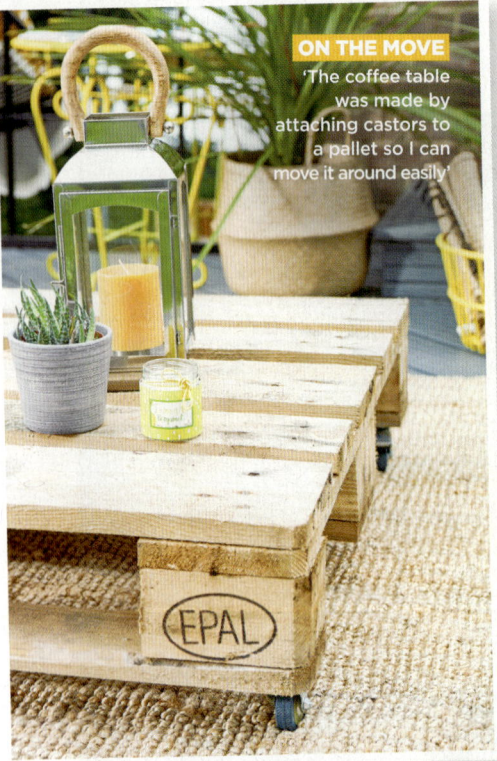

ON THE MOVE
'The coffee table was made by attaching castors to a pallet so I can move it around easily'

'I've gone for a

COME ON IN!

ABOUT ME I'm Katie Blinch and I work in property management. I live in this three-bed house in Turners Hill, West Sussex, with my boyfriend Ben and our two dogs, Chester and Lily.

THE CHALLENGE Although the garden wasn't in a bad condition, it was really bland and boring. A long stretch of wooden decking and a tiny bit of grass was pretty much all there was out there.

THE WISH LIST I wanted to create a relaxed seating area, so we painted the decking and edged it with a rope rail to zone it. Then I went for lots of mismatched boho-look furniture to create a bright, homely feel.

zesty BOHO VIBE'

'I've teamed vibrant lemon and lime colours with jute, seagrass and macramé accessories. The hanging chair is from eBay – we love sitting out here as it's such a fun, sociable space'

Wanting to inject her outside space with a burst of sunshine, Katie turned her bland garden into a bright, relaxed setting

When Ben and I moved into our home in West Sussex we weren't really sure what to do with the garden, so we left it for a while and got on with decorating the house,' says Katie. 'It's a rental property but luckily the landlord was fine about us changing the decor, so we carried on until finally we turned our attention to the outside space.

The problem was that it had a long stretch of decking and a tiny bit of grass, but other than that it was quite bare. The decking was a light wood and it all just felt a bit boring and not very us. I did think about removing some of the decking to give us more lawn, but if I'm honest, neither of us is a keen gardener so we thought it'd be better to keep it and just add extra plants and pots instead.

Pinning down the look

We didn't want anything too formal – it needed to be a spot we could enjoy sitting out in together to enjoy the sun, and also for barbecues when friends and family come over. I liked the idea of having a mix of furniture rather than anything too matchy-matchy, and as budget was a consideration I thought this might be easier to help keep costs down.

Looking on Pinterest helped me realise the types of gardens I was drawn to, all of which seemed to have more of a boho style, with furniture that wasn't too traditional. Finally, I had a vision of how the space could look!

Painting starts

The back of the house needed a lick of paint, so I went for a fresh white and then chose a contrasting dark grey colour for the decking – it took ages to do, to make sure it was all covered properly, »

TOTAL £1,289

TURN OVER FOR MY SHOPPING LIST

>> but it instantly looked better and seemed more finished.

Furniture fun

Next came the best part – shopping for furniture! I bought a string chair from QVC and teamed it with something that had been on my wish list for a while: a hanging chair from eBay. It's now my favourite part of the garden. I needed a new dining table and when I saw this one, which came with rattan chairs, I knew it would work perfectly with this look. I also bought a huge parasol from ManoMano to keep it shaded when it's really hot – it's a really good size and covers the whole table when it's up, but folds down really neatly. It's probably my best buy and we use it a lot as I don't like eating with the sun beating down on me.

Next up was the hunt for an outdoor coffee table and I struggled at the start, as all the ones we looked at were just really small – and because the deck is quite a large area, I needed something more substantial. In the end, we made one from a pallet and put it on castors, so we can wheel it wherever we need it. It's ideal for this area and a great size.

Finishing touches

Choosing accessories was easy – Homesense was my first port of call and I went for lots of lemon and lime colours on the cushions to make it more zesty and zingy. I like all the yellows and greens which bring a bit of colour to the decking. We spend so much time out here now, having barbecues and just enjoying the space – I wish I'd done it sooner!'

Where to buy Katie's style

Valspar Pure Brilliant White smooth **masonry paint**, B&Q. Ronseal Decking Rescue **paint** in Slate, Screwfix. For a similar **dining table,** try Miami dining table, John Lewis & Partners. For similar outdoor **dining chairs**, try Richmond, VonHaus. Outsunny 3m Banana **parasol**, ManoMano. Outdoor Black arch garden **mirror**, Homesdirect365, is similar. **Metal stand frame**, and macramé hammock **swing chair**, both eBay. For a similar **firepit**, try Steel firepit brazier, The Farthing. Tectake black **string chair**, Robert Dyas. Yellow **side table**; yellow **planters**; **cushions**, all Homesense. Lohals **rug**; Fejka **hanging plant**; Fejka **fern**; Fladis **basket**, all Ikea. **Plants**, from a selection, Dobbies.

WHATEVER THE WEATHER
'The pergola's retractable canopy means we can enjoy the sun or be shaded from it on very hot days'

IDEA TO STEAL
'Hook festoon lights vertically down the wall to brighten a dark corner'

Do it! STYLE AN OUTDOOR SPACE

✴ **CHOOSE FURNITURE AND ACCESSORIES** in materials that suit your scheme. For Katie's boho look, macramé – like the hanging chair and hanging plant holders – works well, as do accessories in jute, rope, hessian and raw wood.

✴ **TREAT YOUR GARDEN** like an outdoor room. Items such as rugs and mirrors work just as well outside as they do in. 'I'd seen lots of outdoor mirrors online and couldn't resist this one,' says Katie. 'It looks like a window and reflects our small bit of lawn, making the space feel bigger.'

✴ **KEEP NICE AND SNUG** on summer evenings. As well as having a basket with throws in to hand, a firepit is a great investment to keep you warm as the evenings cool down. 'We've got a grill for our firepit and we use it to barbecue and toast marshmallows, too,' says Katie.

'I WANTED THE GARDEN TO BE AN EXTENSION OF MY STYLE – SOMEWHERE INFORMAL, FUN AND LAID BACK'

MIRROR, MIRROR
'The large mirror is a real statement piece and makes the space look bigger'

TROPICAL VIBE
'Lots of floor cushions make the space feel cosy and provide fun seating for guests'

STASH & STORE

Tongue and groove storage chest, Waltons

ADD AN 'OVERFLOW' CONTAINMENT UNIT

If your shed or garage is already bursting at the seams with gardening tools, then think about supplementing it with a standalone store where you can stash key pieces, such as folding furniture, cushions or bulky children's toys. Position it close to the house so that the contents are easily accessible and easy to tidy away at the end of the day.

Variera plastic bag dispensers, Ikea

STORE SPORTS KIT

Try an easy Ikea hack for storing games equipment. These rigid tubes (above) are designed for storing plastic bags, but make an ideal home for tennis racquets, cricket bats and golf clubs. Attach to a wall in a line or fix a couple on the back of the shed door for easy access.

Garden
SOLUTIONS

Get a grip on garden clutter with these storage ideas that will get you organised

When the weather's warmer, the garden becomes the hub of family activities, from the kids playing out to meals eaten alfresco. As family life moves outside, the garden can become home to lots of extra 'stuff', from cushions, blankets and outdoor toys and games, to picnicware and barbecue kit.

Finding a handy spot to store seasonal extras and protect them from the elements is a must. Consider stealing back some shed or garage space with a dedicated storage area for outdoor belongings, or if you'd prefer something nearer to the house there are plenty of smaller standalone options that won't eat up too much patio space. Just make sure it's big enough to house all your items.

Elfa garage starter kit, Store

Kolbjorn outdoor cabinet, Ikea

NEAT & TIDY

'CHOOSE CLEAR BOXES FOR STORING SMALLER ITEMS SO YOU CAN EASILY SEE WHAT'S INSIDE AND LABEL THEM TOO'

LISA FAZZANI, EDITOR

KEEP ESSENTIALS HANDY

Save yourself a trek to the shed every time you need something with extra storage positioned closer to the house. Perfect for a patio area, these neat weatherproof cabinets can be lined up against a wall and come in handy for storing cushions, seat pads and gardening equipment, or utilised for stowing picnicware and barbecue gear near an outdoor dining area.

Acacia wood garden bench with storage, Belliani

GO FOR AN UNDERSEAT STORAGE SOLUTION

Keep cushions, throws and seat pads to hand, rather than bundling them into the shed every evening. This garden bench has a lift-up seat with a storage area underneath, making it super-easy to throw things in if there's a sudden downpour. Alternatively, go for modular seating that you can set up to suit your space with underseat storage for cushions.

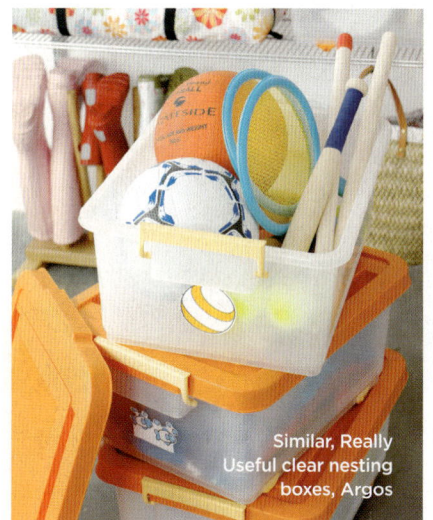

WORK THE WALL

If you've a good-sized garden shed or garage, then consider a dedicated set up for outdoor kit. Wall-hung adjustable shelving can be arranged to suit specific needs, with a combination of shelves, racks and hooks so items can be hung up and floor space left clear. Brilliant for big things like bikes, with smaller items stashed into boxes.

STACK 'EM UP

Children's games and toys quickly get muddy and mildewed if left outdoors in the rain, while hot sun will fade textiles and weaken plastic if heat is extreme. Organise smaller play items into easy-access stacking storage boxes so little ones can find what they're after speedily. Go for clear plastic so the contents are easily visible or label them with images of what's inside.

Similar, Really Useful clear nesting boxes, Argos

Try a speedy
STYLE UPDATE

Entertain in style this summer with cheap and cheerful ideas to brighten up your outdoor space

1 *Pick a floral centrepiece*

Go big with table decorations if you're celebrating a special occasion outdoors. In-season blooms will add a splash of colour to a plain table and if you pick a selection of foliage and flowers from the garden, it won't cost a thing. Stand a hurricane lantern with candle at the centre of your arrangement to take it from day to evening. Use mini jars filled with water around your lantern to hold flowers (rather than using florists' foam) and let them spill over so the base is concealed.

2 MAKE FABRIC POT COVERS

Try disguising plastic planters or tatty terracotta pots by making a few inexpensive fabric cover-ups. Use fabric remnants in a mix of ginghams, florals, stripes or plains – or if you have a stash of rarely used tea towels, put them to good use instead. Cut fabric to size, so that there's plenty to wrap around the pot and enough extra so you can tuck hems in (rather than sewing). Secure in place with garden twine tied in a bow.

3 BRIGHTEN UP A GARDEN TABLE

Looking for a fast fix to cover up a shabby garden table? Why not say it with flowers by throwing over a cheery floral fabric? To cut costs, buy an inexpensive remnant of floral chintz or colourful oilcloth cut to size, or look in local charity shops to find floral curtains you can upcycle into a table cover-up. Don't worry about cutting to size or sewing, let the fabric pool on the floor for a more sumptuous effect.

If space is tight, opt for a circular garden table so you can squeeze more guests around it

4 *Elevate your display*

Make the dining area look extra special so it can be the focal point of outdoor celebrations. A line-up of potted plants along the centre of the table adds instant impact. Go for in-season blooms like geraniums that are cheap to buy so you can use plenty of them. Add height with an overhead arrangement of paper pom-poms or coloured balloons strung across the table. Strings of fairy lights will brighten the area after dark.

5 ORGANISE TABLEWARE

Make it easy for guests to help themselves when you're entertaining a crowd outdoors. Organise cutlery into sets of knife, fork and spoon and then wrap them up individually in a colourful napkin. Pop each set into a clear highball tumbler and line them up beside plates at the end of your serving table. Guests can then pick up everything they need in one go when they're heading over to the buffet.

Make it easy for guests to grab cutlery and go

String festoons above the table to continue the party after dark

6 Raise the bar

In a small garden or compact patio area, make better use of available space by opting for a bar-style seating set-up with a high table and stools, which can tuck neatly underneath, instead of a regular dining table arrangement. Perfect when entertaining, a longline table makes a great social spot for guests to gather around at parties or can do double duty as a bar-cum-serving station stocked up with drinks, cocktails and a colourful array of plastic glasses. Go all-out by hanging a neon bar sign as a fun finishing touch.

Alps pebble six-seat bar set, Dobbies

7 *Keep drinks chilled*

Make ice last for longer in an ice bucket with a few easy tricks. Start off by using a lighter-coloured container – light colours absorb less heat than dark, so ice won't melt so speedily – and the bigger the ice cube, the slower it will melt, too. Position the cooler out of direct sunlight if you can and try lining it with aluminium foil – the reflective surface keeps the temperature more consistent so ice remains cool and intact. And adding a few handfuls of salt to the ice helps lower the freezing point so it will last longer.

MAKE EASY TABLE DECORATIONS BY RECYCLING GLASS JARS AND FILLING WITH POSIES OF FLOWERS – GUESTS CAN TAKE THEM AS A KEEPSAKE AFTERWARDS

Fruit print plates; fruit shaped plates; tumblers; plastic wine glasses, all B&M

8 SET THE SCENE IN STYLE

Go all-out to impress your guests with a fully-loaded table bursting with colour. Inexpensive picnicware looks more lavish when layered up plentifully – go for a mix-and-match look by teaming plains with pretty patterns and set against brightly coloured table runners. When it comes to a table centrepiece, fresh flowers and fruit are cheap to buy and bring an instant hit of colour – stack citrus fruit in clear glass bowls or pile high on platters, or arrange vibrant flowers informally in jugs and pitchers along the centre of the table.

9 Set up a drinks station

If you've lots of guests to cater for, consider setting up a makeshift bar area that can be stocked with cold drinks. Invest in a couple of drinks dispensers filled with ready-made punches so that guests can help themselves and take some of the pressure off the host. Opt for summer classic thirst quenchers, such as Pimm's and lemonade, or non-alcoholic iced tea and fruit squashes. Stock up with plenty of glasses and ice in the freezer beforehand.

PLAN FOR ALL WEATHERS IF YOU'RE HOSTING A PARTY – HAVE GARDEN PARASOLS OR A POP-UP GAZEBO ON STANDBY THAT YOU CAN HEAD UNDER IF IT RAINS

Palm Leaf garland; Tropical Palm Lemon napkins, all Talking Tables

10 MAKE EASY PALLET TABLES

Take a more informal approach to seating a crowd with picnic-style pallet tables lined up on the lawn. Pallets are often readily available and after a quick spruce-up to make sure they are clean, free of sharp edges and any loose nails, can be arranged to make a low-level buffet table. Line with paper table runners and add picnic rugs and floor cushions for guests to sit on.

FEATURE LISA FAZZANI PHOTOGRAPHS FUTURECONTENTHUB.COM SUSIE BELL, DAN DUCHARS, POLLY ELTES, WILLIAM GODDARD, WILLIAM SHAW, PELARGONIUM FOR EUROPE

Use to store drinks, stools and accessories when not in use

BAR

Forest wooden garden bar, Shedstore. Anthracite Grey wood paint Thorndown

11 GET THE PARTY STARTED

Invest in your own back garden cocktail bar so you can entertain friends and family outdoors all summer long. Easily constructed from a flatpack kit, this combination timber bar-cum-shed has an open-out serving hatch to make a bar for garden parties, but can be closed up to store garden furniture and equipment over the winter months. Paint the exterior timber a dark shade for a chic look, with the interior in a paler colour for contrast, then fill with glasses and cocktail-making essentials for a glitzy look.

Outdoor solar lanterns, Sparkle Lighting

12 *Add sparkle after dark*

Ensure that you can party on into the evening by organising plenty of outdoor lighting for the garden and patio area. Up the wow factor with a cluster of colourful Moroccan-style lanterns suspended above a dining table or seating area. Hang from the branches of nearby trees or fence posts if you can, with extra lanterns dotted along the table or close by. Solar-powered lights are a good option as they require no additional wiring in and will charge on standby throughout the day. Position to illuminate pathways and steps after dark.

'It's our own

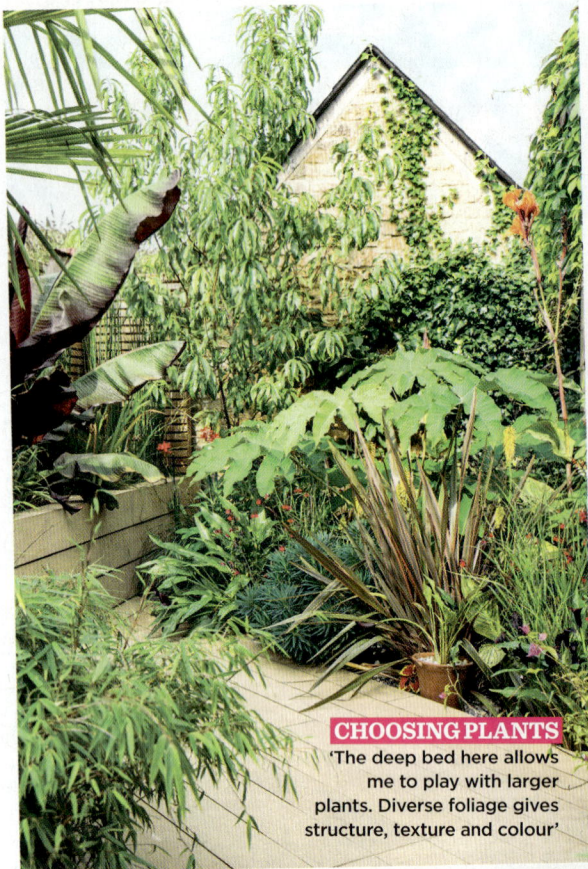

CHOOSING PLANTS
'The deep bed here allows me to play with larger plants. Diverse foliage gives structure, texture and colour'

COME ON IN!

ABOUT ME I'm Emily Crowley-Wroe, a garden designer (april-house.co.uk), and I live here with my husband Shaun and daughters Eve and Eleanor, in a 1880s five-bedroom, semi-detached, listed house in Bourton-on-the-Water in the Cotswolds.

THE CHALLENGE Our L-shaped rear garden had broken fence panels and was pretty empty and devoid of atmosphere.

MY WISH LIST We wanted a garden full of exotic plants, along with an area where we could place furniture or exercise.

SPLIT LEVEL
'The raised dining space is framed by a green-oak pergola with beams in one corner for a swing seat. If we have people over, we can move the table to the main area'

TROPICAL OASIS'

Faced with a drab garden, Emily decided to fill it with exotic plants, vibrant colour and a flexible outdoor living area

When we moved house in 2017, we realised the rear garden had been glossed over in the particulars,' says Emily. 'It had broken fence panels, depressing flagstones and some sad-looking pots. It needed to be given a new lease of life and some personality added to it. Luckily, I began studying garden design in 2018, so the timing was right to use our own garden as a case study for the course.

Perfect vision

I knew I wanted an outside room that felt spacious and connected to the modern rear of our house, with lots of exotic plants that would transport us somewhere far away and dreamy... a complete contrast to the cottage garden at the front. I started developing my wish list, which included having an area where we could eat, several spaces to sit and pockets of planting that would be roomy enough for some big feature plants to add atmosphere to the garden.

Next steps

Once I was sure about what I wanted to include, I set about factoring in where everything should go. I surveyed the space, which included measuring the boundaries in relation to the house, noting the position of the sun throughout the year, checking the soil type and drawing a scale plan to create the new design. It's an important part of designing an outdoor space and something that really helps make a garden a success.

Focus on plants

I also made a separate plan for the planting, which was equally important as this helped me decide where to put each plant depending on its growth habit and whether it likes sun or shade. For our garden, I looked for hardy exotic ▶▶

TOTAL
£8,800
TURN OVER FOR MY SHOPPING LIST

LOTS OF LAYERS
'Having raised beds and ground-level beds means I can add height and create a layered look. It's easier to maintain raised beds and there's less digging into compacted ground, too'

TOP TIP
'An outdoor rug adds colour and helps define a seating area'

Do it! PLAN YOUR GARDEN LIGHTING

✳ There are four different types of lighting when it comes to outdoor spaces: ambient (to add atmosphere), task (so you can see to barbecue or read), security (for safety and to deter intruders) and feature lighting (to bring your garden to life).

✳ To begin with, decide on the areas you want to light and what your key features are. Will you need more light in your cooking and eating areas, for example? Do you have steps or a steep incline that you'll need to illuminate?

✳ Vary heights, from floor lanterns and floor spots set into decking, to overhead pendants, wall lights or a canopy of twinkly fairy lights.

✳ Highlight areas of the garden, such as trees or borders, water features or sculptures. LED spike spotlights can be pushed into the ground and angled upwards, or combine two or three spotlights for an elegant result.

✳ Add drama by positioning lights so that they make an exciting feature of your trees and foliage after dark.

FEATURE KATE HILL PHOTOGRAPHS LIZZIE ORME

IDEA TO STEAL

'Potted plants can be moved for seasonal variety in the planting and decking areas'

SEATING AREA

'The hanging chair offers a more relaxed way to spend time outside – plus it's easy to store away in winter'

'THE ATMOSPHERE OF THE GARDEN, BOTH DAY AND NIGHT AND EVEN IN THE RAIN WITH THE SOUND OF DROPLETS ON THE BIG LEAVES, IS WONDERFUL'

» plants in complementary colour combinations with striking foliage.

Maximising space

As the garden is just 57 square metres, I decided to deck the whole space and add a mix of planting beds and raised beds for height. The decking is laid on a 45-degree angle to make the space feel larger, especially in the narrower part of the garden. Cutting the boards at an angle was time-consuming, but this was key to making the garden feel more expansive, and we added lighting in the area where there's a step to make it safe at night.

That's not the only lighting either – we also added a pergola and strung fairy lights above it, along with a few lanterns dotted about on the decking.

I chose a bright turquoise dining set, along with a hanging chair, and chairs and a coffee table for another seating spot. I went for vibrant colours, and added outdoor rugs and tropical-look cushions.

Year-round fun

The transformation took four weeks and we spent £8,800, not including the labour. Even though it's a small garden, we have plenty of space for a multitude of activities all year round. We've had nights around the fire pit, yoga and HIIT sessions and we have also discovered that it makes an excellent dance floor!'

Where to buy Emily's style

For similar blue **chairs**, try Acapulco in Blue, Homebase. For a similar **swing seat**, try Reelak, La Redoute. For a similar outdoor **rug**, try Green Decore, Robert Dyas. For similar orange **chairs**, try Southbury 2, Wayfair. For similar **lanterns**, try Bloomsbury lantern candle holders, John Lewis & Partners.

Discover more handy tips on creating a smart garden at Instagram / @styleathomemag

STYLISH SHELFIE
'Chris used leftover wood from the worktop to make floating shelves to fit in this small, awkward alcove'

'It's the island

IDEA TO STEAL
'Bold colours won't make the room dark if you accent with lighter tones'

COME ON IN!

ABOUT ME I'm Celie Horton, a lead clinical paramedic practitioner and I live with my husband Chris, a welder fabricator, and our two dogs Rogue and Logan, in our three-bedroom semi-detached cottage in Ullesthorpe in Leicestershire, built in 1878. We bought it in September 2019, although we didn't move in until December.

MY CHALLENGE We started with the kitchen and top of our wish list was an island. We also wanted to make the most of the views at the back of the house.

MY WISH LIST We knew we wanted bifold doors to enjoy views of the fields, as well as a Belfast sink and, of course, that all-important island.

OF OUR DREAMS!'

'I'm a big fan of bold colours so blue units were a natural choice. As it's a strong colour, we've kept the walls and tiles light, and we chose a white quartz worktop'

Celie and Chris knew exactly what they wanted for their kitchen renovation, but convincing the designers was a bit of a challenge...

We're both originally from Birmingham but decided to move to the village of Ullesthorpe in Leicestershire for a slower pace and better quality of life,' says Celie. 'We've always enjoyed creating things, but did minimal renovations in our first home, which we bought when we were in our 20s – it was mainly just redecorating. However, we did convert a van into a camper van, which is where we got the bug for renovation.

We love the history that comes with this property – it was built in 1878, and is opposite a milestone. It's known that whoever lives in the property is called the 'keeper' of the milestone – hence my Instagram handle @milestone_cottage.

Chris actually purchased the house without me seeing it. I was on a trip and when I came home, he said he'd found a house that he wanted us to view. At the end of the viewing he confessed that he'd already bought it! Thankfully, it paid off as I'd already fallen in love with the potential of the place.

Coming up with a plan

The kitchen was one of the first jobs we tackled. The original space was quite small, so we knocked the wall down into the room next door, which created a long narrow space where we could fit bifold doors. My kitchen wish list had always included an island, but we had to go to three different kitchen designers before we found one who was able to make our dreams a reality. We were originally told that because the kitchen was long and thin there wouldn't be enough room for the island... thankfully they were wrong! Our fab designer at Wren was able to create exactly what we wanted, and ❯❯

TOTAL £8,780

TURN OVER FOR MY SHOPPING LIST

➤➤ we chose a Shaker-style kitchen in blue. Best of all, the price included the sink, appliances and pre-assembled units, as well as the quartz worktop.

Chris was planning to do most of the work, but with a four-week delivery time, we had to quickly prep the space ready for fitting, which involved ripping out the old kitchen, chiselling off floor tiles and boarding, plastering and whitewashing the space. Chris was then able to fit all the units and appliances – he's been brilliant, turning his hand to everything and saving us a fortune.

Worktops, tiles and floor

We went for white quartz-style worktops, with a contrast wood section on the island. I found some fabulous hexagonal wall tiles with a linear pattern that look great against the units and we used them on the wall behind the cooker as a focus.

We found original timber flooring in some of the other rooms, so I was keen to keep the kitchen floor similar. We chose a parquet design, which also picked out the wood on the island. I liked the idea of exposed brickwork, too, so we used these fabulous wall tiles to create a feature area at the other end of the room.

Styling it up

As we wanted to keep the look clean and uncluttered, I've been reluctant to add too many accessories, but the velvet bar stools, a bargain buy, are one of my favourites and the velvet complements the blue units. I also wanted a statement light above the island, and found this one online, with its pretty handblown glass finish. It gets lots of compliments.

I'm thrilled with how the kitchen has turned out and our first home-cooked dinner after months of microwave meals was glorious, especially as we could sit at the island and appreciate the view.

Where to buy Celie's style

Infinity Shaker **units**, **appliances** and **sink**, Wren. Treviso **worktop**, Stone Worktop Specialists. Flavel **cooker**, Argos. **Tap**, eBay. Palm Springs Hex **tiles**, Metro Tiles. Pipes Bar **ceiling light**, Comet Lighting. Hexagonal mosaic **tiles**; Manhattan Rustic brick-effect **tiles**, both Total Tiles. **Walls** in White emulsion, Dulux. Thorpe Roasted oak herringbone **flooring**, Luxury Flooring & Furnishings. Tiffany **bar stools**, JTF Mega Discount Warehouse.

COOL CONTRAST

'I couldn't be happier with the island and I love the fact the overhang has been finished in a different surface'

IDEA TO STEAL

'Create an overhang on your island so it can double up as a breakfast bar'

WALL PLAN

'These rustic wall tiles give the room a focus point and tie the room in with the wood-style parquet flooring'

'I'M THRILLED WITH HOW THE KITCHEN TURNED OUT – AND OUR FIRST HOME-COOKED DINNER AFTER MONTHS OF MICROWAVE MEALS WAS GLORIOUS'

Do it! TILE A WALL

1 Prep the wall by removing dust and dirt, and ensuring it's dry.

2 Mark vertical and horizontal lines on the centre of the wall being tiled using a pencil and a spirit level. Lay your tiles out starting from the middle and working your way out towards the edge of the wall.

3 Apply tile adhesive, starting from the central vertical line. Firmly press the tile into the adhesive using a slight twisting motion. Position a tile spacer between each tile on all sides.

4 Tiles can be cut with a score and snap tile cutter. For irregular cuts, such as around plug sockets, a diamond wheel tile cutter is a good idea. Allow the tiles 24 hours to dry.

5 Apply grout using a rubber float or squeegee, pressing firmly into the gaps. Wipe away excess with a damp sponge, being careful not to remove from the grout line itself.

6 After about 30 minutes, buff the tiles with a soft, dry cloth to remove any trace of grout.

FEATURE ZOE BISHOP PHOTOGRAPHS LIZZIE ORME

Smart ideas for
KITCHENS

Six stylish and practical projects to update and organise your kitchen

Six peg oak shaker rails, Yester Home. Hanging Nalbari pizza board; Kiko Brass photo frames; Mina hanging terrarium, all Nkuku

Hang a wall-to-wall peg rail

Utilise a cabinet-free wall by creating hanging space for kitchen essentials – chopping boards, jugs and mugs, for example – while dispersing decorative bits and bobs like hanging plants and picture frames between them.
Give it a twist Paint a strip of colour below the rail to frame the objects.

Revamp a cabinet with glass film

Use sticky backed plastic to transform a plain kitchen cabinet into an up-to-date storage piece. The film will also help to prevent chips and scratches.
Give it a twist Replace the fluted film with a frosted or patterned, stained glass-style alternative.

Keep the look modern with a plain white granite surface and matching splashback

Solyx reeded glass adhesive film (on cabinet doors), Glass Films

Natural cork wall tiles, Portuguese Treasures. Mini buckets, Hobbycraft

Stencil numbers in the corners with black paint

1

2

Upcycle an old window frame

Create a handy kitchen noticeboard by fixing cork tiles on to the back of an old frame using a glue gun or strong tape. Screw hooks into the bottom edge for mini buckets and attach to the wall with strong fixings. **Give it a twist** Add a splash of colour by painting the cork a bold shade or create a pattern effect.

A vintage loaf tin doubles as a fun planter

Try Anaxagore hanging shelf, La Redoute. For similar lamps, try Jesper Industrial style hanging lamp, Lights.co.uk. Cabinets painted in Black Blue, Farrow & Ball

Add a ceiling-hung shelf

Make space on your surfaces while ticking the style box by hanging a shelf from ceiling brackets – the perfect place to grow fresh herbs and store unused vases.
Give it a twist If ceilings are high enough, attach large cup hooks to the underside to hang pots and pans and free up cupboard space.

Keeping the walls, shelves
and cabinets all the same
colour will allow vases, urns
and artwork to really pop

For similar clear glass
vase, try LSA International
Flower kiln vase, John
Lewis & Partners. Turkish
urns, from a selection at
Etsy. Tribeca rimmed
cereal bowls, M&S

Add a subtle, slimline shelf

Continue the bottom line of your
wall cabinets with a narrow
streamlined shelf, perfect for adding
a cute area to display artwork,
photos, postcards and fresh foliage.
Give it a twist Attach a brass
hanging rail to the base of the shelf
for mugs and utensils.

White gloss units are the perfect foil for this geometric monochrome splashback

Black grid mesh panel 60x120cm, Ukpos.com. White bowls with Blue rim, Falcon Enamelware

Create a wire rack splashback

Cut a wire rack to size and attach to the wall using small cup hooks, leaving a 10mm gap between the wall and the racking to accommodate the S-hooks.
Give it a twist Add some colour to your kitchen by spray painting the racking a bright shade.

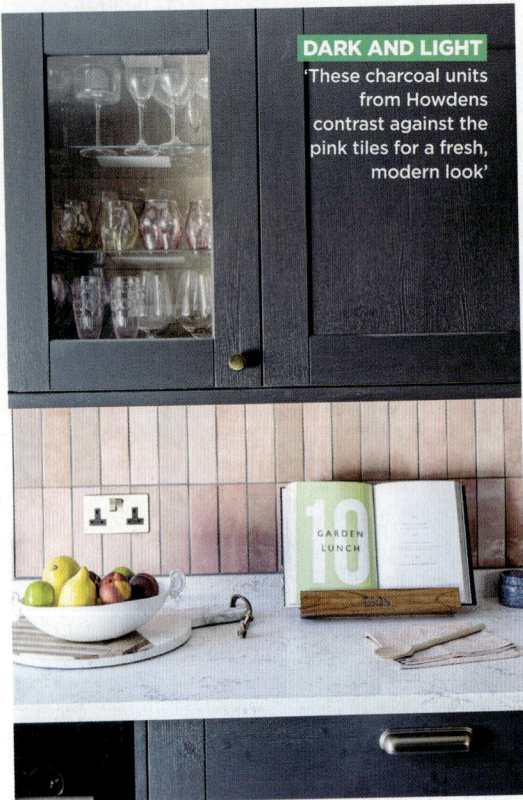

'Pink wall tiles

COME ON IN!

ABOUT ME I'm Gemma Daley and I live here with my husband Daryl in our three-bedroom Victorian terrace in Brighton. We moved here in June 2020 – you can find us at @house. with.the.purple.door.

THE CHALLENGE The kitchen was dated with beige units and brown worktops. There was a small back door and tiny window, so this room always felt dark and dingy.

THE WISH LIST We knew clever design choices could make this space look cool and edgy, for example by injecting colour into the room with pink wall tiles. I'd always wanted a pantry so we had to come up with a clever way to add this.

DRAMATIC TRANSFORMATION
'Renovating our kitchen was a top priority. We wanted to turn this room from dark and dated into a bright and modern space'

add a COOL EDGE'

'Choose full-width metal-framed doors to allow daylight to flood into a kitchen space'

Gemma remodelled her dark, gloomy north-facing kitchen into a bright and cheerful space that is packed with tonnes of unique ideas

When we bought our Brighton home in June 2020, it was a renovation project and every room needed updating,' says Gemma. 'At the top of our to-do list was transforming the bland kitchen, which had beige units and dark worktops. It didn't seem to matter how sunny it was outside, the room always felt dark and gloomy. Our idea was to install huge glass back doors and a new, larger window that would allow daylight to filter into the room – as well as fit a brand new kitchen.

We hired our friends, who are contractors, to undertake the building works. The first thing they did was rip out the old units, appliances and floor. They also pulled down an internal wall to open up the under-stairs cupboard, and they knocked out the back wall to make a bigger opening for the large glass doors I'd been dreaming of.

Unexpected delays

Unfortunately, our house renovations started at the beginning of lockdown and we were hit by Covid restrictions and building supply issues. What we had originally hoped would be a speedy project, ended up taking over nine months to complete.

We set up a makeshift kitchen in the living room and we ate lots of takeaways, living with a half-finished kitchen for weeks on end. Eventually the dust and mess got too much for us and the house became uninhabitable so we moved in with family.

Our kitchen project was hit by unexpected delays. The longest gap we faced was waiting for the window and doors, which took eight weeks longer than planned. Our home was freezing »

TOTAL £9,757

TURN OVER FOR MY SHOPPING LIST

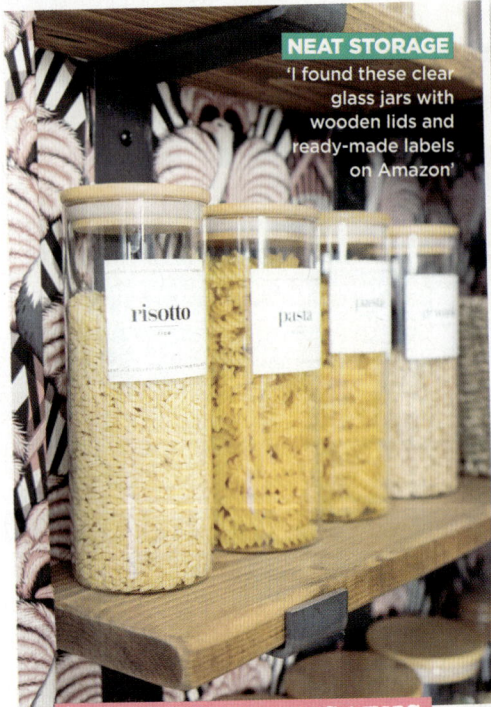

NEAT STORAGE
'I found these clear glass jars with wooden lids and ready-made labels on Amazon'

IDEA TO STEAL
'Show off your best accessories with open shelving'

'THIS HOUSE IS GOING TO BE OUR FOREVER HOME, SO WE THOUGHT IT WAS WORTH BUYING DECENT FITTINGS THAT WOULD LOOK GOOD FOR LONGER'

Make it! DIY JAR LABELS

✳ **CHECK YOUR CUPBOARDS**
You don't have to invest in a set of storage jars. Save money by repurposing attractive containers like empty jam jars or glass bottles.

✳ **CLEAN THEM UP** Remove old labels by placing them in the dishwasher or by soaking them in hot water with washing-up liquid. Or you can even use a hairdryer to heat up the label, making it easier to peel off.

✳ **GET CREATIVE** There are several ways you can create matching labels – either download a free template or design them yourself, and then stick in place using glue.

✳ **MAKE IT PERSONAL** Or, if you have neat writing, you can use white oil-based pens to write directly onto the glass. That way you can update the label to match the contents as needed.

LASTING CHOICE
'Inspired by kitchens I had seen on Instagram, I chose the pink and black colour palette for a look that would last'

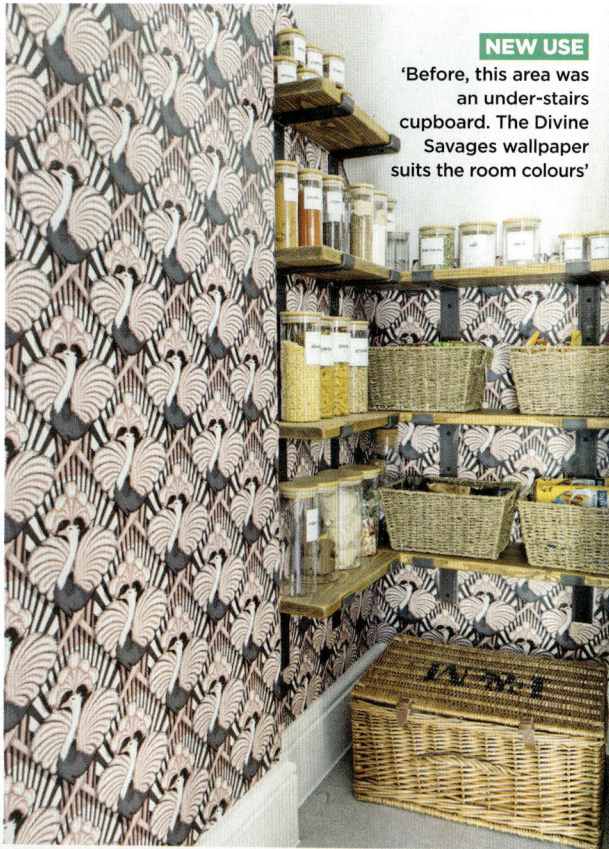

>> because we had a temporary back door during the winter months. And when they were finally fitted, we found out our dream kitchen was out of stock, which caused further interruptions.

Sticking to the design

My inspiration for the colour scheme for our new kitchen came from Instagram where I'd seen lots of pink and black kitchens. I spent ages hunting down the perfect charcoal Shaker-style units, so when my kitchen went out of stock, it was frustrating. But rather than go for another style or colour, we decided to wait. I didn't want to compromise because I knew I'd regret that decision in the long term.

To save money on the project, we sourced the units, tiling and appliances ourselves. This got a bit tricky at times as halfway through tiling the walls, we realised that we didn't have enough pink metro tiles. I had a mad dash across town to pick up a couple of extra boxes. Luckily, they were still in stock.

In the end, we decided to upgrade our appliances and invest in better quality worktops. This house is going to be our forever home so we thought it was worth it as they'd look good for longer.

Last touches

Once our builders were finished, it was time to focus our attention on the finishing touches. We turned an awkward corner into a clever pantry area and I unpacked my collection of accessories to dress the kitchen shelves.

I'm so pleased with the end result. All the details that we have added to this space, like the metal-framed doors, the casement window, the pink tiles and the pantry, have injected lots of personality into our kitchen. It's completely unique to us.'

Where to buy Gemma's style

Fairford 600 3-drawer base **unit** in Charcoal, Lamona ceramic butler **sink**; Lamona swan-neck **tap**; Contessa aged brass classic round **handles**, all Howdens. For a similar **worktop**, try Calacatta Imperial Quartz, Gemini Worktops. For similar **floor tiles**, try Stoneage Lux Grey Porcelain Semi Polished floor tile, 600x600mm, Tile Mountain. Artesano Rose Mallow 6.5x20cm **wall tiles**, Tiles Direct. Zsa Zsa Candy **wallpaper**, Divine Savages.

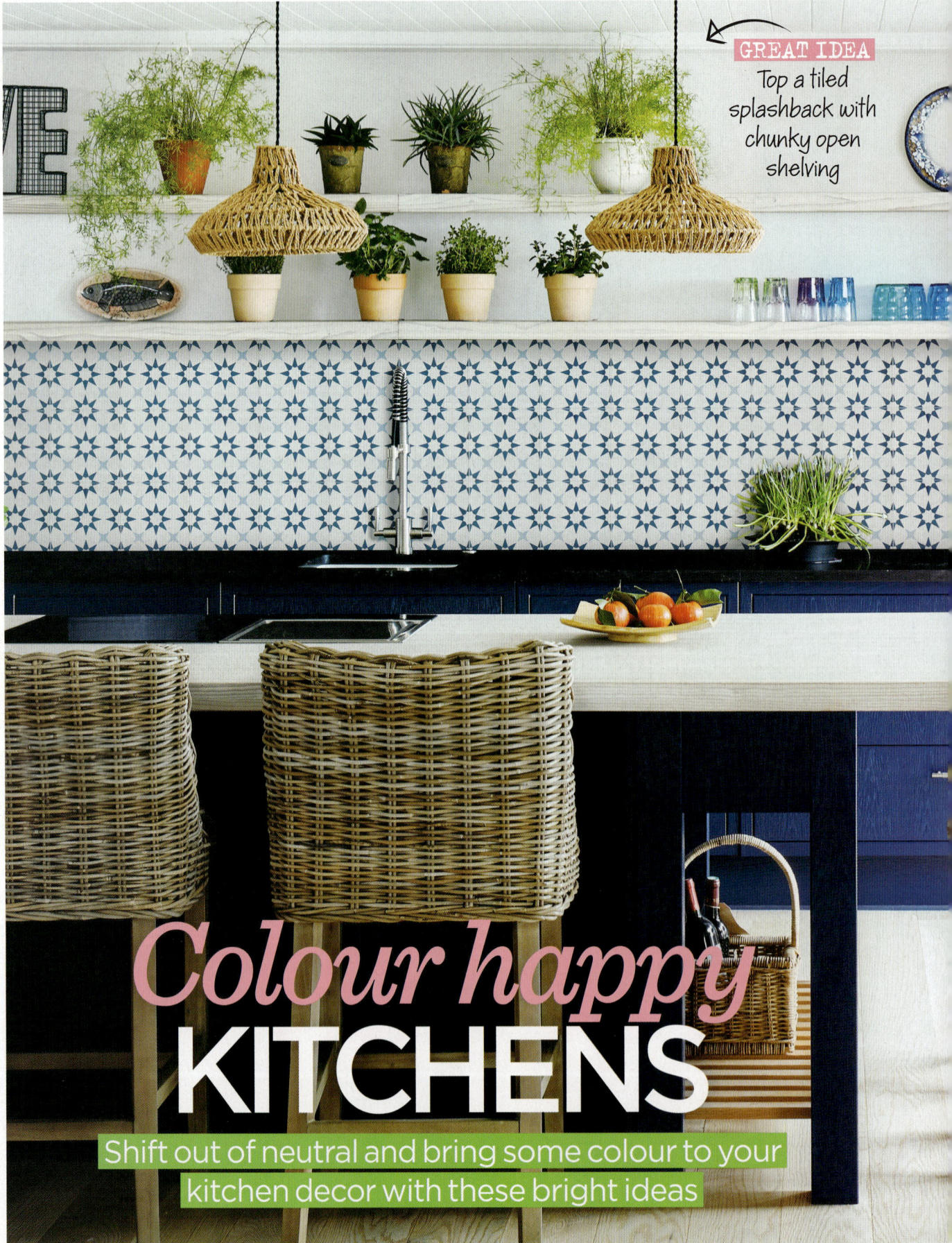

GREAT IDEA
Top a tiled splashback with chunky open shelving

Colour happy
KITCHENS

Shift out of neutral and bring some colour to your kitchen decor with these bright ideas

Make a statement with a striking print – this wallpaper splashback is waterproof and heatproof. Flower and marble splashback, Limelace

Perk up plain units with a tiled splashback in a playful pattern. Atlas Porcelain Blue tiles, Ca' Pietra

Use... *a statement splashback*

Make instant impact with a show-stopping splashback that'll add colour, pattern or texture to kitchen walls

✳ **CREATE CONTRAST** Splashbacks are a great way of bringing extra personality and colour to a plain kitchen. Go bold by choosing a glossy tile or glass splashback in a contrasting colour that stands out from the cabinets.

✳ **PLAY WITH PATTERN** Replacing the splashback is an easy way of revamping a tired kitchen that needn't involve a whole refit. Tiles are great for adding a pop of pattern that can lift a plain scheme visually. Pick a repeat design, such as a lively geometric or a rustic Mexicana-style tile to add a playful touch.

✳ **GO FOR A ONE-OFF** For bigger impact, consider a bespoke splashback. Try mix-and-match patterned tiles to create a patchwork effect or use decorative tiles or painted panels to create a pictorial frieze.

✳ **THROW SOME SHAPES** Instead of patterned tiles, use unusually-shaped tiles, such as a hexagonal or scalloped shape that will create a patterned effect and give a visual lift. Alternatively, create pattern by laying tiles in a herringbone or chevron format or stack metro tiles vertically rather than horizontally.

Create a graduated effect with cabinets in tonal shades. Parallels Ashton Grey and Cloudy Grey kitchen, Superfront

Use... *colourful cabinetry*

Let your kitchen units steal the scene, by choosing pretty pastels, standout brights or even a two-tone colour combo

✳ **GIVE YOUR KITCHEN A GLOW UP**
Cabinetry is often the first thing you notice about a kitchen, but while wood finishes and neutral colourways are a safe choice, there's nothing like a standout colour to give your kitchen the wow factor. In north-facing spaces add warmth by opting for mood-boosting yellows, soft oranges or blush tones.

✳ **EMBRACE CALM SHADES** Softer shades like mint, pink, powder blue and grey can look super-smart on kitchen cabinetry. Steer clear of sickly-sweet shades and go for grey-toned pastels for

a grown-up feel, teamed with luxe brass or bronze door handles and drawer pulls.

✳ **MAKE IT HALF-AND-HALF** Can't decide on a colourway? Mix it up by using a two-tone colour combination. Colour wheels will help you find your perfect match, but a good rule of thumb is that if they have the same undertone they should work together.

✳ **TRY A QUICK CHANGE** Take a more flexible approach by choosing painted cabinets. Colour choice is unlimited and if you want to change the colour later, cabinets are easily repainted.

Go for warm, sunny colours to create an upbeat vibe. Chilcomb paintable kitchen, Howdens

GREAT IDEA

Use lighter tones on surfaces to create areas of calm

Kitchen tips and tricks

❋ **PLAY WITH COLOUR** Large kitchens with lots of natural light can accommodate brighter tones and darker colours without being overpowered. Use colour samples to get a feel for how colours will look at different times of the day.

❋ **TONE DOWN** Offset colourful kitchen units by teaming with light-coloured worktops. Pale colours can make a space feel brighter by reflecting any light.

❋ **THINK SMALL** Work extra colour into a scheme with appliances and colourful ceramics.

Kitchen tips and tricks

✱ **LIGHTEN UP** Choose a dark colour for the kitchen island and low cabinetry, with upper cabinets in a lighter shade. A paler colour on top will draw the eye upwards and make the space feel loftier.

✱ **CHANGE TACK** Contrasting end or back panels can offer extra depth and dimension to a kitchen island, whether in a bold colour, glossy finish or in a textured timber.

✱ **TAKE A SEAT** For an easy colour fix, go for upholstered bar stools in a plush fabric or bold colour that will pop against a plain island.

GREAT IDEA
Utilise end-of-unit space by adding a handy bookshelf

Go for gold accent panels to add a touch of luxe. Soprano large pendant light, Pooky

Bring some softness to a steely scheme with a standalone island in a soft blush pink. The Slab Collection kitchen in Dry Rose and Graphite, 1909 Kitchens

Use... *an eye-catching island*

The island is at the heart of the kitchen, so make it unmissable by opting for a bold colour or standout finish

✳ **CREATE A FOCAL POINT** Choosing a kitchen island in a contrasting colour to the units will ensure that it stands out more prominently. With neutral-coloured kitchen cabinets, choose a bold shade to set the island apart. And vice-versa with dark or brightly coloured units, go for an island in a muted or neutral tone so it won't compete for attention.

✳ **ADD AN ACCENT** Matching island colour to kitchen cabinets is a good way of creating continuity in an open-plan space where there's lots going on. Try adding a contrasting back panel on an

island to bring in a subtle pop of colour and create a visual resting place.

✳ **WRAP IT UP** Opt for an on-trend look with a kitchen island 'wrap' that involves taking a stone or composite worktop all the way down the sides of the island too. Also known as a waterfall edge, it adds a luxe finish and looks striking in a contrasting colour to cabinets.

✳ **MAKE IT EYE-CATCHING** Go for a standout back panel to make a freestanding island the star feature. Tiles make a practical finish and are a great way of adding pattern and colour.

Restrict pattern to a small-scale design if matching splashback and floor. Hoxton tiles, Wickes

Use... *focal point flooring*

Put the focus on the floor in a busy kitchen with smart flooring options that combine style and practicality

✳ **COMBINE DESIGN AND DURABILITY**
Porcelain tiles are super hard-wearing, waterproof and easy to keep clean and with the wide range of colours, patterns and shapes available, offer plenty of decorative scope in a kitchen area.

✳ **GO BOLD WITH PATTERN** Make a feature of kitchen flooring with a patterned design that grabs your attention as you enter the room. Be led by the style of your kitchen or period of your property for decorative inspiration, whether you opt for traditional Victorian geometric tiles for a classic look, or

make it modern with a vibrant colour in a shapely format or interesting layout.

✳ **COMPLEMENT KITCHEN SURFACES**
Choose designs that complement each other, whether tiles in the same pattern but in a different scale, or using tiles of the same colour but in different shapes.

✳ **SET THE PACE** A change of flooring is a clever way of creating different zones in an open-plan space. To make the transition between kitchen and dining areas, try teaming patterned tiles with plain or use contrasting colours to visually separate the two zones.

Pick a pattern with similar colour tones to complement cabinets. Lisbon Flora patterned tiles, Porcelain Superstore

GREAT IDEA
Choose a glossy finish to set off plain white tiles

Kitchen tips and tricks

✳ **IN THE ZONE** If a patterned floor is too busy, use a small amount of pattern with a border around an island or the edges of the room instead. It will help draw attention to a shapely feature.

✳ **GO FAUX** Vinyl is a great alternative to tiles. Softer and warmer underfoot, vinyl has plenty of look-alike options that mimic the effect of timber or tiles.

✳ **CHANGE DIRECTION** Lay tiles in different formats to enhance a space. Square tiles laid in a diamond format will add width.

FEATURE LISA FAZZANI

'We relocated

COME ON IN!

ABOUT ME I'm Kate Maunders, head of marketing at Primark, and I live here with my husband Phil, a solicitor, and our two cats, in a two-bed Victorian semi in Essex, which we bought in 2015.

THE CHALLENGE Our bathroom was originally on the ground floor at the back of the house, so after living with it for a few years we turned an upstairs bedroom and loo into the new bathroom. It needed designing from scratch.

MY WISH LIST A freestanding bath, separate walk-in shower and a double vanity were the priorities, and as our old bathroom had been really dark I wanted this one to be nice and bright.

TOTAL
£6,042

TURN OVER FOR MY SHOPPING LIST

our BATHROOM'

Faced with a dark, dated downstairs bathroom, Kate was keen to create an upstairs layout that was luxe and light

IDEA TO STEAL

'Leave windows free from dressings to maximise light'

W hen we moved into our house, the bathroom was originally downstairs and although it was a good size, it was quite dated, with brown tiles and brown walls,' says Kate.

'We lived with it for around four and a half years while we did other works to the house, but we always knew we'd relocate the bathroom upstairs eventually.

Changing rooms

We began to plan the new layout, and decided to turn the existing downstairs bathroom into a snug, with doors out to the garden – and it made sense to do all the work at once. Although we knew the old bathroom hadn't been fitted well, it was only when we ripped out the bath that we found out it had been leaking into the floor and sub floor for years!

Upstairs, the new bathroom was going to take the place of what was a bedroom and separate loo. Thankfully this meant we already had the plumbing in place. I played around with the layout for a while to make sure we were optimising the space, using an online planning tool from B&Q, which was helpful as it brought the design to life on screen.

Luxe looks

There were a few key items that I wanted to include, such as a freestanding bath, walk-in shower and a double vanity, which would give us all the storage we needed. I'm so glad we went for this, rather than a single vanity, as with the mirrors above it makes the space feel like a luxury hotel.

I've always been drawn to classic, timeless decor with a modern twist, so I went for marble tiles on the floor and walls, but then added a modern-look metal-frame shower cubicle.

I also wanted the space to feel light, in stark contrast to the bathroom »

SET IN STONE
'I'm glad we went for the large-format marble floor tiles rather than something smaller – they emphasise the amount of space in this bathroom'

HANGING OUT
'We made sure the heated towel rail was close to the bath, so it's easy to grab a towel when you get out'

'USING AN ONLINE PLANNING TOOL WAS REALLY HELPFUL – IT BROUGHT THE BATHROOM DESIGN TO LIFE'

FEATURE LAURIE DAVIDSON PHOTOGRAPHS LIZZIE ORME

» downstairs, which had been really dark. We chose a paint called Smudgewand from Fenwick & Tilbrook for the walls, which is a soft dusty pink colour and looks great against the white tiles.

Work begins

The builders started by knocking down the wall between the bedroom and loo to create the new bathroom space, then took up the floor to install the new plumbing. When the floor came up, however, we found that the floorboards underneath were in really bad condition. It meant we needed a whole new floor, which was costly. Thankfully that was our only hiccup.

With the bedroom and loo having been knocked through, it meant there was a "nook" behind the door as you come into the room. We did consider having the shower there, but decided to position the loo there instead, which means it's nicely tucked away. The work took around four weeks in total and we had a carpenter come in to install some floating shelves for us too.

Bargain shopping

As I knew when the work on the bathroom was kicking off, I was able to buy a lot of the bigger items during a sale period, which helped keep costs down.

When it came to accessories, I found some sweet storage boxes and toiletry trays from Primark Home, along with lots of candles and diffusers from its home fragrance range. The towels are from Next – the soft pink goes well with the walls.

I'm proud of how this room has turned out and I absolutely love the space – it's even better than I'd hoped it would be.'

Discover more handy tips on creating a smart bathroom at **Instagram /
@styleathomemag**

IDEA TO STEAL
'Black fittings add a modern look to a timeless scheme'

Where to buy Kate's style

For similar bath, try Newham freestanding **bath**; Trent Black freestanding **mixer tap**; Trent **mixer taps**, all Bathroom Mountain. Piana double **vanity unit with stone basin**, Lusso Stone. Milano Nero Black thermostatic **shower with round shower head**, Big Bathroom Shop. Mode Black framed shower enclosure with stone **shower tray**; Orchard Eden close coupled **toilet**, all Victoria Plum. Vellamo Matt Black **mirrors**; for a similar **heated towel rail**, try Crosswater MPRO Matt Black, all Drench. **Walls** painted in Smudgewand pure matt, Fenwick & Tilbrook. Carrara White matt marble porcelain wall and floor **tiles**, Tile Mountain. Zellica Antique **wall tiles** (in shower), Topps Tiles. Lucide Scott **wall lights**, Lighting Direct. **Scent diffuser**, **storage baskets**, **soap dish** and **trinket tray**, from a selection, Primark Home.

LIGHT TOUCH
'The wall lights are from Lighting Direct and are modern without jarring with the classic look'

WATER FEATURE
'The shower head from Big Bathroom Shop is a really good size – we could get away with it as it's a spacious room. I love the little alcove for toiletries too'

TUCKED AWAY
'It's nice that the loo is out of the way in a little nook. We had the shelves above it built to fit'

USE WALL SPACE

Form Cusko Grey floating shelf, B&Q, is similar

STORE AND DISPLAY

The area running along and above a bath can be put to use quite easily. Avoid full-depth shelves that might obstruct headroom; instead opt for a narrow floating shelf or slimline ledge that will keep bathing essentials to hand and provide space for displaying items.

White floating shelf, Homebase, is a match

SLOT INTO A GAP

Boxed-in plumbing and pipework can leave awkward nooks and crannies in bathrooms that often get left unused as standard-sized furniture won't fit. DIY shelves make a neat option that can be cut to size and simply slotted in and are perfect for stashing towels and loo rolls, or used to hold mini baskets and caddies filled with toiletries and make-up.

Bellwood over-the-toilet storage unit, A Place for Everything

Space-saving BATHROOM STORAGE

Bring order to a small bathroom with these neat ideas and compact storage solutions

Keeping small bathrooms ordered and tidy can be a challenge. Lack of space often leaves little extra room for storage, meaning that surfaces get cluttered with toiletries, and rails and hooks overloaded with damp towels and bulky bathrobes.

Space-saving furniture and multi-tasking storage pieces are a must when bathroom space is tight or there's a danger of the space feeling even more crowded and chaotic. Look out for slimline shelves and units that can squeeze into small gaps or slot in beside baths and shower cubicles. Or utilise wasted wall space with clever racks and rails over doors or neat shelving units that are designed to sit under wash basins or above the loo.

Ivar side unit
(used as a towel
ladder), Ikea

PROP IN PLACE

TAKE IT TO THE WALL

Extra-tall, slimline storage can work super well in a small bathroom, slotting into tight gaps at the end of the bath or next to a basin and utilising wasted wall space. Try this easy hack using an Ikea shelving side unit that doubles up as a longline towel ladder that simply props against a wall for instant extra hanging space.

Raskog trolley,
Ikea

MOVE IT AROUND

A compact storage trolley is perfect for a tiny bathroom, fitting into the smallest of spaces and on castors so you can easily move it about the space as needed. Perfect for housing bathing essentials, stash towels and washcloths on the bottom shelves and toiletries at the top so you have all your must-haves instantly to hand.

'KEEP FLOORS AND SURFACES AS CLEAR AS POSSIBLE IN A SMALL BATHROOM – CLUTTER WILL MAKE THE SPACE FEEL MORE CROWDED'

LISA FAZZANI, EDITOR

Over-door
multi shelf
unit, Next

GO OVER AND ABOVE

Wall space above a loo often gets left unused, but in a small bathroom where space is at a premium, it's a prime spot for squeezing in extra storage. Go for a freestanding over-the-loo shelf unit that simply stands against the wall, leaving the loo area unobstructed but with shelf space above for storing loo rolls, and other bits and bobs.

UTILISE DOOR SPACE

Make use of wasted space behind a bathroom door with a slimline rack that hooks over the top edge of the door. With shelf space for small bottles, plus hanging room underneath for towels, it requires no screws or fixings so can be easily moved if needed. Racks that hook over a shower panel or cubicle are another similar option.

FEATURE LISA FAZZANI
PHOTOGRAPHS FUTURECONTENTHUB.COM/OLIVER GORDON, CAROLYN BARBER

Try a speedy STYLE UPDATE

Bring colour into your life with these cheap and cheerful ideas to brighten up a boring bathroom

1 *Create a chequered floor*

Breathe new life into shabby bathroom floorboards with a smart chequerboard paint effect. You'll need a neutral base as your starting point – either natural timber or painted boards are fine – with the tile effect created in a brighter contrast colour. Use a pencil, tape measure and masking tape to mark out and line up the area to be painted and then fill in your top colour with a small brush and roller, working in alternate rows. Leave to dry and apply another coat if necessary. Once thoroughly dry, seal with clear lacquer to protect.

Chalk paint in Old Violet, Annie Sloan

Contour Navy Palm Leaves wallpaper, B&Q

2 GO BIG WITH A BOLD WALLPAPER

While regular wallpaper isn't recommended in damp, humid spaces, specialist bathroom wallpaper is designed to cope with steamy conditions. Contour wallpaper has a 3D effect that can be used to mimic the look of tiles, marble, mosaic or simply to showcase an eye-catching print (like this botanical) and has a splashproof and wipe-clean finish.

Bath painted in
Dorchester Pink deep
intelligent eggshell,
Little Greene

*Choose a blind with
a bold plant print
to complement the
botanical vibe*

3 PAINT THE BATH A PERKY SHADE

Grab the attention in a small bathroom by painting the bath an eye-catching colour. Whether you have a classic freestanding bath that could do with an update or a more modern fitted bath with timber cladding, both can benefit from a lick of paint in a cheery, uplifting shade. Clean and prep the exterior surface before painting. Cast iron and acrylic baths will need a thin coat of an appropriate primer (as will timber panelling), then once fully dry, apply two top coats in your chosen colour.

Wall painted in Niagara Blues 4,
Sincere Brew and Bleached Lichen
3 mixing easycare bathroom soft
sheen paint, all Dulux

4 *Have a go at ombré stripes*

Make your bathroom a relaxed and restful retreat by choosing a calming colour scheme of beach-inspired shades. Paint the walls in wide bands of subtle colour, ranging from sand and pebble tones on the lower section, to sea blue and cool grey on the upper section. Blur the effect by painting wavy edges rather than straight lines, which will look softer and easy on the eye. You can then continue the coastal theme with shell, pebble and driftwood accessories, teamed with sponges, loofahs and natural greenery.

5 PUT THE FOCUS ON THE FLOOR

While using glossy white wall tiles and fittings can help to stretch the space and make a small bathroom look bigger, having no colour at all can sometimes feel quite harsh and clinical. Look to the floor instead and add a splash of colour with patterned floor tiles or a bright bathroom vinyl. Used across a small area, bold flooring will be less pricey and putting the focus underfoot helps to draw the eye outwards and make the area feel more spacious. Repeat the tile colours around the bathroom on towels and accessories for a co-ordinated look.

Wall in Cobalt Night, Drifting Cloud and Grey Splendour mixing easycare bathroom soft sheen paint, all Dulux

Amberley Orchid floor tiles, Topps Tiles

Paint an accent stripe to add interest

6 Go dark with stripes

Having a smaller bathroom doesn't mean that dark colours need to be avoided. Opting for an all-dark colour scheme can add a sense of drama in a small bathroom and bring a feeling of depth and warmth. Painting the ceiling a dark colour is another good tip for any small room, which will help to elevate the space by leading the eye upwards. Paint bands of graduated colour on the wall using two dusky shades separated by an accent stripe in a lighter tone.

7 Change direction with tiles

Classic brick-shaped tiles are an ever-popular option for both bathrooms and kitchens, that lend themselves to a variety of pattern formats and styles. As an alternative to the more regular horizontal brick-style layout, stacking tiles in a vertical format, as pictured here, can help to elongate the space and make a low-ceilinged bathroom feel taller and more lofty. Go for soft, muted colours to create a sense of calm, with grout in a toning shade that blends in rather than stands out.

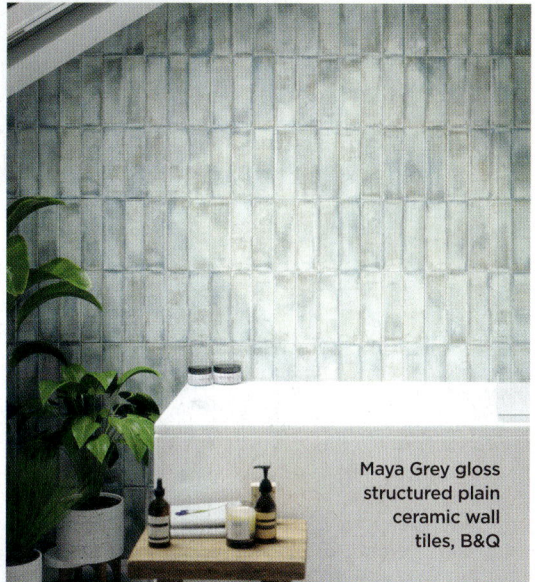

Maya Grey gloss structured plain ceramic wall tiles, B&Q

'PLANTS ARE A BRILLIANT WAY TO ADD LUSH COLOUR. ALOE VERA, MONSTERA AND BOSTON FERNS ALL THRIVE IN HUMID CONDITIONS'

Orchard square edge bath; back to wall loo; pedestal basin, all Victoria Plum

8 COLOUR-BLOCK WITH BATHROOM TILES

Whether your bathroom is large or small, colour-blocking is a fun technique that can be used to highlight different zones, such as the bath and shower area, or around a wash basin or loo. Similar to painting coloured blocks in a living space, the effect is easily recreated in a bathroom using panels of coloured tiles for a more practical and waterproof finish. Start with a neutral backdrop on walls and floors, then pick two or three contrast colours for block areas of tiling.

9 Stencil a floral splashback

Plain tiles offer a brilliant opportunity for getting creative and adding a bold pop of colour to a dreary bathroom for very little cost. As long as the existing tiles are in a decent condition, painting over them is an inexpensive way of brightening them up and a good stop-gap solution if you're intending to replace tiles further down the line. Choose a stencilled floral design for an eclectic look or opt for repeat geometrics for a simpler effect. Coat the tiles with a primer before stencilling in your chosen design. When dry, apply clear tile sealant on top to protect your paintwork.

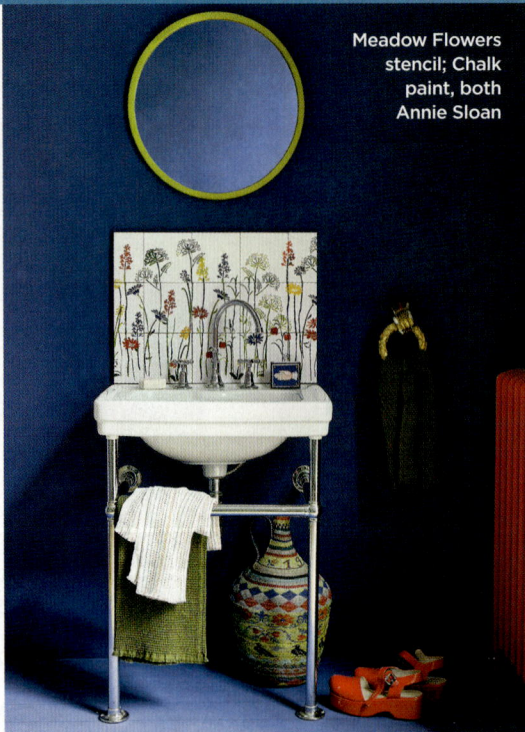

Meadow Flowers stencil; Chalk paint, both Annie Sloan

'FOR A MORNING ENERGY BOOST, PAINT WALLS IN WARM REDS, ORANGES AND YELLOWS; SOFT GREENS AND BLUES CREATE A CALM AND RELAXING VIBE'

A water-resistant blind is durable and can deal with humidity levels

10 SWITCH TOWELS FOR A CHANGE OF SCENE

A super-easy idea, but one that can have a big impact in any bathroom, is simply replacing old bath towels and bath mats with new. Sort through threadbare or mismatched towels and switch things up with a fresh set of towels in a chic, co-ordinating colour palette. Pick a design and colour that complements your scheme, whether soft greens with neutrals, or bright geometrics and patterns to add pep to a plain bathroom scheme.

Brixton towels in Khaki, Christy

11 GO FOR A BOLD BLIND

The window is the perfect opportunity to add a large area of colour and pattern to a bathroom, which can help to brighten a plain scheme. Choose a simple roller blind, rather than fussy curtains or a pleated fabric blind. For steamy bathrooms, water-resistant polyester rollers are practical as moisture simply slides off the surface. For windows that come into close contact with water, such as next to a shower or bath, go for PVC roller blinds which are fully waterproof and thicker for greater privacy.

Valspar Kitchen & Bathroom matt paint in Devonshire Green, B&Q

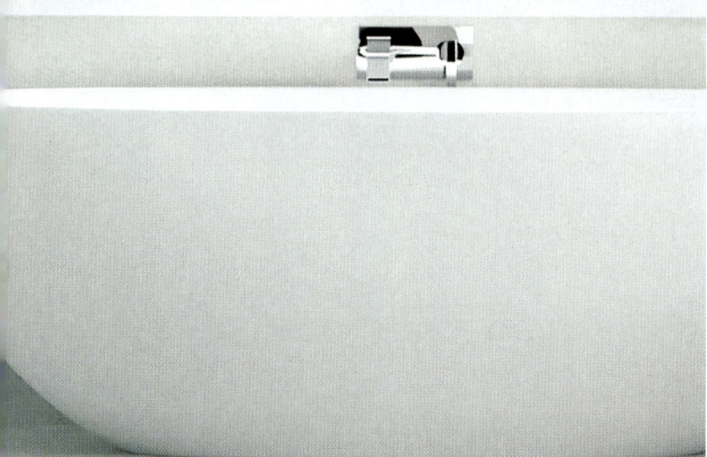

Splash Blackout Two Colour Stem roller blind, Blinds 2go

12 *Create a focal point*

Narrow bathrooms can feel quite long and corridor-like if not treated carefully. Painting the end wall a dark, standout colour is a clever way of creating a focal point that draws the eye in, squaring off the space for a more evenly balanced look. Emphasise the effect further by filling the wall with eye-catching artwork, a collection of wall mirrors, or simply add a set of bathroom shelves styled up with decorative ornaments, beauty buys or lush greenery.

FEATURE LISA FAZZANI PHOTOGRAPHS FUTURECONTENTHUB.COM

CHANGE IT UP
'I love rearranging the objects on display for a new look'

COME ON IN!

ABOUT ME I'm Claire Douglas (clairedouglasstyling.com). I live with my husband Spencer and children Oscar and Milo, in a 1960s three-bedroom detached house in Tunbridge Wells, Kent. We moved here in summer 2016.

MY CHALLENGE The living room was part of a 1980s extension; it had no central heating and the layout was badly planned. It felt like it had been just stuck on – it wasn't the multifunctional family room that we needed.

MY WISH LIST We wanted to knock down the dividing wall to open the space but our budget couldn't stretch, so we had to think of other ways to make it flow.

TOTAL
£1,985
TURN OVER FOR MY SHOPPING LIST

sion for DIY HACKS'

'Forage branches to make great seasonal displays on your shelves'

SUPER SOFA
'This was once a corner sofa, but I cut the footstool bit off with a saw then glued on wooden beading to decorate the arms and base'

Claire loved the idea of built-in cupboards in the room, but when custom-built proved too expensive, she made her own!

Although this house was in a poor state when we viewed it, we fell in love with its potential,' says Claire. 'The purchase process was tricky – it dragged on for over six months – and the stress just started there.

Our new home was an ex-rental and had been empty for ages. The boiler was beyond repair and the toilets didn't flush! Basically, every room needed urgent attention before we could move in.

The work begins
We had a new boiler installed within days, and the bathroom refitted within a couple of weeks. Next was the kitchen, which we replaced within four months. After all that, it was a couple of years before we had the energy to tackle the other rooms.

Making progress
In December 2018, we started the living room by having bi-fold doors fitted. They instantly transformed the space, letting in natural light and connecting the room to the garden. A long column radiator was installed and we laid new flooring throughout the ground floor.

Getting it right
The changes made a huge improvement, but the room still didn't feel inviting. In hindsight, I'd made the classic mistake of putting the furniture against the walls to make the space feel bigger. I researched furniture configurations to suit the room's shape, then moved the sofa and armchairs to the middle around a coffee table.

DIY and upcycling
Through lockdown I kept busy with lots of DIY projects, which I documented on @instahome_uk. For the living room, I came up with the unusual idea of upcycling a tatty old sofa by covering it in strips of wooden beading. I also »

FEATURE MAXINE BRADY PHOTOGRAPHS DAVID GILES

'IN A RECTANGULAR ROOM, ADD CURVES WITH A ROUND RUG, COFFEE TABLE AND MIRROR TO STOP IT FEELING LIKE A CORRIDOR'

Make it!
REEDED FURNITURE

Claire used this simple trick to add ridged texture and interest to a plain coffee table. You could also try it on cupboard or sideboard doors or other flat surfaces.

✱ Clean your secondhand piece of furniture using sugar soap.

✱ Decide on a design and the effect you want. You could cover the whole tabletop or copy Claire's idea with wide stripes. You'll find a large selection of wooden beading at DIY stores and timber merchants.

✱ Measure and cut the individual strips of beading to size. Stick in place with a multipurpose glue.

✱ Prime the finished piece, then paint it in a colour of your choice. For a more durable surface and to protect your design, you could get glass cut to size for the top.

revamped an Ikea coffee table I picked up on Facebook Marketplace for £10.

Ikea hack heaven

My biggest challenge for this room was making the built-in shelving. I'd dreamed of a wall of bespoke joinery but it was way beyond our budget. I decided to make my own by customising four Ikea Billy bookcases. I transformed them into built-in shelving for under £350.

Obsessed with styling

I'm most proud of the shelving units as I made them entirely on my own. One of the best bits about the open shelves is the opportunity for endless faffing. It's become a running joke in our house that I'm always re-styling my shelves.

The finishing touches

Lockdown and the closure of non-essential shops meant a trip to my beloved HomeSense was out of the question, so I was forced to be a bit more resourceful than usual. Facebook Marketplace was fabulous as it allowed me to source many unusual pieces for next to nothing. I kept my eyes peeled for antique books, vases and ornaments for a mix of old and new.

Getting crafty

I also foraged for greenery and twigs in my garden. I love creating interesting displays on the shelves and walls. I made textured artwork using cheap canvases from an art shop and a tub of filler, which I painted with leftover emulsion.

My room now

My living room is everything I wanted it to be. During the day, it's used as a playroom or I host friends for coffee. On summer evenings, we open the doors to enjoy the garden. I love the space, and it feels bigger with the wall-to-wall shelving, too.'

Discover more handy tips on creating a smart living room at Instagram / @styleathomemag

FRESH FACELIFT
'I gave this old table a new style with beading and a coat of paint'

PANEL SHOW
The simple half-height panelling effect brings a smart dimension to the white walls

IDEA TO STEAL
'Opt for two armchairs and a sofa – it will give you more flexibility with the layout'

WIDE OPEN
'We replaced three old uPVC windows with these new bi-fold doors that really connect the room to the garden'

Where to buy Claire's style

Tub **armchairs**; **bench**; Bamboo **side table**; Anthracite Grey **column radiator**, all eBay. **Paint** shades DCO273 and DCO2001 colour match emulsion, Decorating Centre Online. Click-fit **blinds**, Blinds2go. Tawny Chestnut click-fit **laminate flooring**, Howdens. **Round mirror**, Dunelm. **Wall lights**, Amazon. Lantern **ceiling light**, Wayfair. Tall Green bottle **vase**; Gold **candleholder**; Grey **face ornament**, all Jysk. Black and White **cushions**; Yellow **cushions**, both H&M. Round **rug**, nuloom. Grey **dinner candles**, Tusk Collection. **Reed diffuser**, The Somerset Toiletry Co.

1. Use foliage to blend inside and out

Greenery is a simple way to bring the outdoors in. Whether you're green-fingered or prefer faux, choose a combo of leafy foliage and grasses, in a variety of shapes and shades.

2. Keep the backdrop calm

Choose neutral tones for walls, floors and larger pieces of furniture. A soft pale green on the walls will create a soothing feel, while sandy-coloured upholstery and accessories creates a relaxed atmosphere.

The New Look
INDOORS OUT

Blur the lines between the interior and outside, by using nature's textures and colours in your scheme

FEATURE LAURA HIGGINS

SOFT TOUCH
Faux mohair check throw, Next

3. *Work with naturals*

Use natural materials such as wood, cane and rattan to connect with the outdoors. Wooden floors or cladding creates eye-catching detail. For tables and chairs, choose rattan and unfinished wood.

SPECKLED PATTERN
Green glass organic shaped vase, Freemans

NATURAL BEAUTY
Rattan mirror, Cox & Cox

Nail the style
GENTLE TONES
Mix leafy shades with natural materials

FOREST FEEL
Green Leaf crewel cushion, B&M

BRANCH OUT
Zen chenille Navy flatweave rug, Dunelm

4. *Pick colours from nature's palette*

Take your cue from nature and combine shades of earthy greens, watery blues and natural wooden tones, which will work towards smudging the edges between inside and out, even on gloomy days when the doors are closed.

Green textured vase; Green jug; natural diamond crochet throw; Riverside glass vase; natural woven wood basket; natural woven seagrass mirror; Blue willow leaf cushion; Green cord cushion; Green check throw; embroidered shape cushion, all George Home

UNDER £260

WOVEN LINES
Wicker two-tone basket, B&M

Cosy looks for
LIVING ROOMS

Turn up the heat with ideas for warm and welcoming
spaces you'll want to hunker down in

GREAT IDEA
'Break up plain walls
with strategically
arranged artwork'

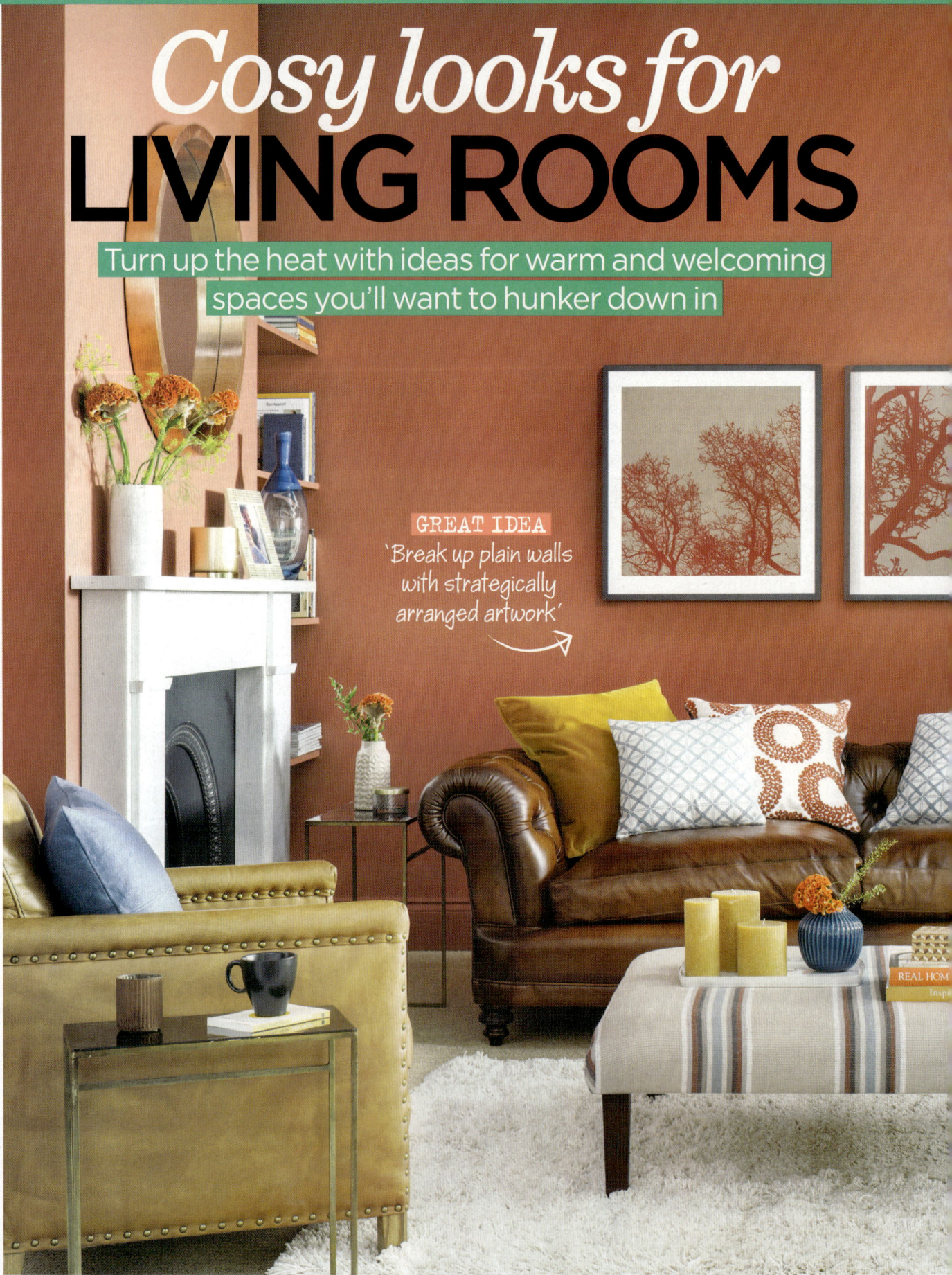

Anchor your living room around an inviting fireplace

Use black and white as accent colours

Try.... *autumnal tones*

Look to deep reds, oranges and earthy terracotta to create a rich backdrop

✳ **BRING SOME HEAT** Shades like russet and terracotta, or more spicy cinnamon and ginger, will add instant heat and warmth to a room. An autumnal palette is the perfect choice for spaces that you retreat to at the end of the day, such as living rooms, TV dens and snugs.

✳ **SET THE MOOD** Painting all four walls in a rich, earthy colour will create an immersive and intimate mood, ideal for rooms where you want to feel cosy and cocooned. In larger spaces, try painting just one wall to highlight the room's focal point, such as a fireplace or sofa.

✳ **SWAP HERO PIECES** Opting for upholstery and soft furnishings in these rich tones is another way to up the cosiness factor in living rooms. Pick key pieces, such as the sofa and armchairs, in a plush fabric or chestnut leather. Or add a statement rug in a spicy shade.

✳ **ADD CONTRAST** With a warm, cosy palette like this, bringing in a contrast accent colour is key, otherwise it can all feel a bit overwhelming. Try pops of black and white with neutrals, such as grey and stone, or go for a zingier mustard yellow or soft denim blue.

Opt for a supersized rug to cosy up smart floorboards

GREAT IDEA
`Keep it subtle, with a feature wall painted in a soft contrast shade'

Try... *tactile textures*

Snuggle up with lots of cosy layers and feelgood fabrics

✳ LAYER IT ON Neutrals are a winner all year round, but when the temperature drops, opting for cosier fabrics and touchy-feely textures is the way to go. Think chunky boucle, thick wool and soft brushed cotton for upholstery or to add an extra layer of insulation at windows.

✳ SNUGGLE UP Extra cushions, throws and rugs are an inexpensive and easy fix when it comes to cosying up living rooms. Swap summer cottons for knitted woollens, chunky weaves, faux furs and fleecy throws layered on sofas, and thick rugs and sheepskins to warm up floors.

✳ GET A GLOW ON Work in warmer accent colours to take the chill off cooler neutrals. Swirl shades of caramel, coffee and tan throughout the living room to bring a soft, cosy glow, peppered with touches of darker chocolate brown.

✳ LOWER THE LIGHTS Rethink lighting choices as the seasons change. Ditch harsh overhead lighting and try a more layered scheme with table lamps, floor lights and wall-hung fixtures. These all cast a more flattering glow that will enhance your room scheme and feel more in sync with the season.

Use accent colours and tactile textures to lift an all-white scheme. Esme Stripe woven cushion; sage bouclé cushion; waffle throw, all B&M

Pick cosy fabrics

✳ GO FOR WEIGHTY CURTAINS
Naturally thicker fabrics, such as velvet and bouclé, do a great job of keeping heat inside, especially when paired with a thermal lining. These fabrics are also excellent noise and light barriers.

✳ ADD A THERMAL LAYER
Thermal linings are an extra insulating layer which can be added to existing curtains or Roman blinds over the winter, to take a room from warm to toasty.

Opt for mix-and-match upholstery choices to create an opulent look. Ralph three-seater sofa; Felix accent chair, both Furniture Village

GREAT IDEA
'Paint walls and panelling the same colour throughout for a luxe look'

Keep in the warmth

❋ **LET IN DAYLIGHT** Open window dressings during the day to take advantage of the warmth from natural sunlight, and close them when the sun sets to retain heat and maintain privacy.

❋ **TRY SMARTER LIVING** With smart technology, you can schedule your electric blinds to lower when the room drops below a certain temperature, all from the touch of a button, an app or voice control.

Give walls a velvety finish with flat matt paint. Dulux Heritage Cherry Truffle velvet matt emulsion, Designer Paint

Try... *plush finishes*

Indulge the senses with an opulent scheme in deep, sultry tones

✳ **MAKE IT SUMPTUOUS** Opting for tactile fabrics, such as velvet, chenille, damask and devoré, is a sure-fire way to up the cosiness levels. With a plushness and warmth that looks and feels ultra indulgent, deep-pile fabrics are also hardwearing and drape beautifully – a great choice for upholstery and curtains.

✳ **PICK LUXE COLOURS** Match the opulence of velvets and chenilles with an equally luxe colour choice. Rich berry, deep reds, pinks and purples lend drama and warmth. Pepper with accents of navy, emerald green or mustard yellow.

✳ **STAY MATT** When it comes to your living room walls, go for all-over coverage in a flat matt emulsion to give a rich, velvety finish. With minimal sheen and depth of colour suited to deep and dusky shades, matt walls look great with skirting and trims painted the same shade for a fabulous immersive look.

✳ **SHINE ON** Bring out the intensity of darker colours with high-sheen accessories to provide contrast. Try a metallic side table and lamps in burnished gold and copper, and shapely ceramics and glassware for extra sparkle.

Go for expertly fitted blinds to keep chills at bay, ensuring rooms stay cosy. Expression Sombre Roman blinds, Hillarys

Try... muted naturals

Bring the outdoors in with soothing shades, from soft green to taupe and cream, for a relaxed, cosy scheme

✱ **CALM WITH GREEN** This versatile colour is a safe option when it comes to living rooms. Cocooning in the winter and cooling in the summer, muted-green shades of the countryside, such as sage, moss, olive and khaki, will create a relaxed mood that feels calm and restful.

✱ **BRING BALANCE** All schemes need neutrals to create balance. Echo outdoor colours by teaming earthy greens with plenty of natural materials, from tactile stone and timber to tanned leather and burnished metals. Pair green with browns to bring out its warmer tones.

✱ **INTRODUCE PATTERN** Muted shades can merge into one if not done carefully, so bring in a pattern or two to add visual interest and lift an all-natural scheme in an instant. Look to leafy prints on wallpaper, curtains and soft furnishings, teamed with tweedy woollens and stripes, heathery checks and plaids.

✱ **DO THE DETAIL** Well-chosen finishing touches are what pulls any room scheme together. Stick to the natural theme with foliage, plants, pottery and ceramics, combined with wooden details on furniture, picture frames and ornaments.

GREAT IDEA

'Arrange artwork in a grid format to fill wall space above a sofa'

Set a tan leather sofa against a leafy wallpaper backdrop for a nature-inspired scheme

FEATURE LISA FAZZANI **PHOTOGRAPHS** FUTURECONTENTHUB.COM/ CLAUDIA BRYANT, DOMINIC BLACKMORE, CAROLYN BARBER

Try a speedy STYLE UPDATE

Get creative with easy ideas to brighten up your bedroom that won't cost a fortune

1 *Revamp a dressing table*

Give a shabby piece of furniture a new lease of life by repainting it a jazzy new colour and adding sparkly drawer pulls and a mirror. Find an old dressing table or wooden desk at a charity shop or online. Start off by lightly sanding to get rid of rough edges and flaky paint, then wipe over with a damp cloth. Depending on which paint you choose, the surface may need priming first to give a longer lasting finish, then simply apply one or two coats of your chosen top coat in a bold, standout colour. Finish with some new handles.

Peacock eggshell emulsion paint, Dunelm

2 DISPLAY PICS ON LEDGES

Mosslanda picture ledges, Ikea

Create an easy-change picture gallery to go above a bed. Using narrow picture ledges means that any artwork you choose can be easily updated – unlike pictures that are fixed to the wall. Go for four or five ledges, arranged at staggered heights so you can style them with an assortment of different-sized pictures and small decorative pieces. Include one or two larger pictures in your display to give the look balance.

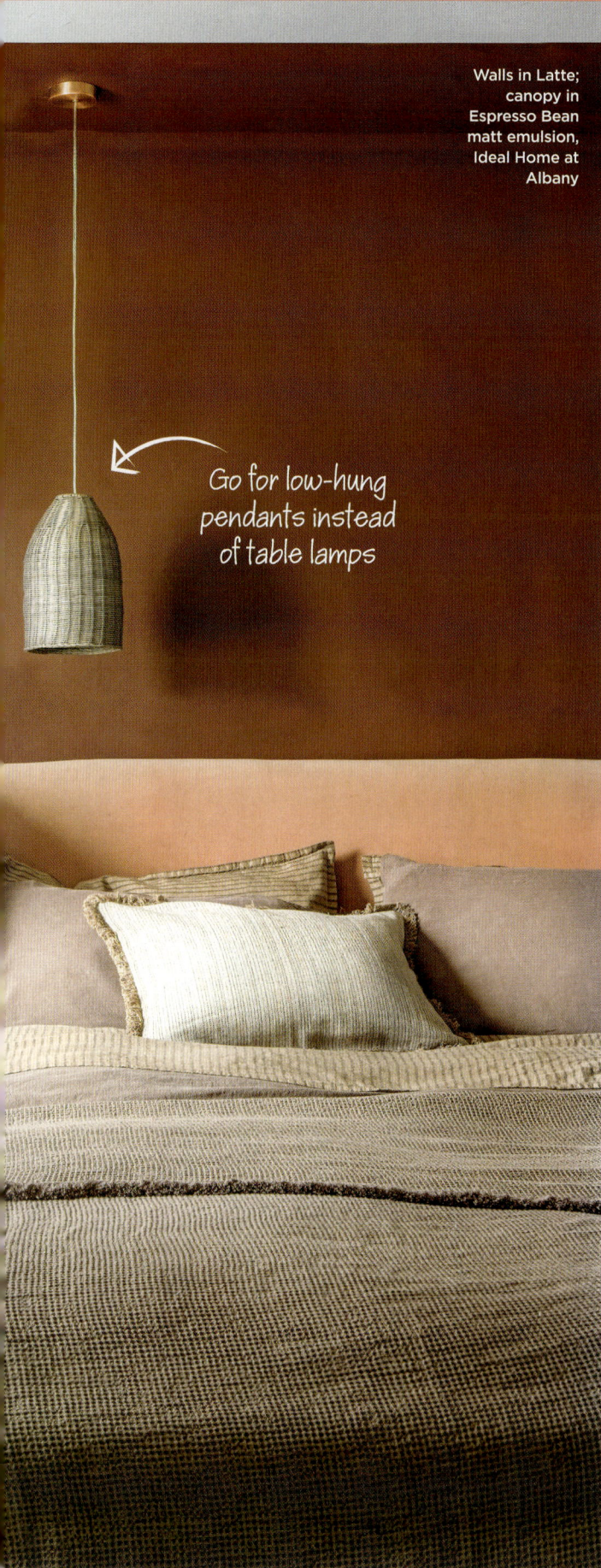

Walls in Latte; canopy in Espresso Bean matt emulsion, Ideal Home at Albany

Go for low-hung pendants instead of table lamps

3 PAINT A CANOPY ABOVE THE BED

Make the bed the focal point of the bedroom with a painted canopy that wraps the area in colour for a cosy, cocooning effect. Start with a paler shade for your main wall colour, with a darker complementary shade for the canopy. Decide how far you want the canopy to extend onto the ceiling first – try a shallow canopy like this one for ease or continue over the whole length of the bed for extra impact. Use decorator's tape to mask out the area to be painted.

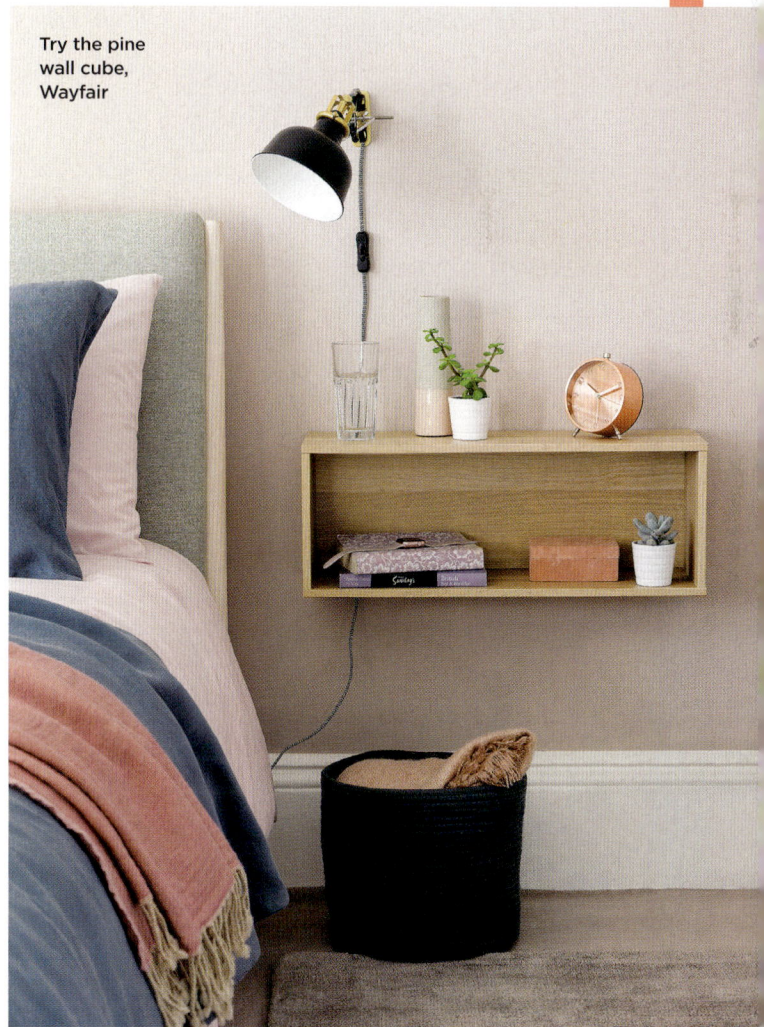

Try the pine wall cube, Wayfair

4 *Save space with a bedside shelf*

If bedroom space is tight, go for wall-hung bedside storage rather than bulky tables. Wall-mounted storage is neat and compact (with no legs to get in the way) and helps create the illusion of extra space by having the floor underneath on show. Neat box-style shelving is cheap to buy or simple to put together and gives shelf space for books and essentials, plus room for a few extras on top. Adding wall-mounted lights instead of bedside lamps will also free up extra surface space.

5 TRY A FAUX 'PEARL' EFFECT

Upcycle an unloved item of bedroom furniture with paint and turn it into a glam statement piece. Perfect for an old chest of drawers or cabinet, this clever stencilled paint effect creates the look of inlaid pearl. Using chalk paint, decide on your dark base colour first – black, grey or navy will create contrast that will make the 'pearl' effect stand out. Then give your furniture one or two coats and once dry, use a stencil and white paint to create the overlaid effect. Seal with a pearly glaze to add shimmer.

For a similar look, try Shaker style peg rail, The Dormy House

Chalk paint; Pearlescent Glaze; Annie Sloan

6 Combine storage and display

Extra storage is always welcome in a bedroom and this clever peg rail idea looks super stylish too. Running the entire width of the room or downsized to just a smaller section, it will provide hanging space for essentials, as well as creating a display area for more decorative pieces. Position at picture-rail height so that items are easily reached but won't get in the way, and either go for natural wood against a contrast background or paint the peg rail to match the walls.

Hang florals or fragrant foliage above the bed

7 *Wrap up your hottie*

Make an easy cover for a hot water bottle using a piece of thick felt. Cut the felt to size, so it is the same height as the bottle and wide enough to wrap around and overlap by about 4cm. Stitch on two buttons with wool yarn, leaving a length of yarn that can be wrapped around the buttons to secure it. Sew a fabric pocket on the front which can be filled with calming dried chamomile or lavender.

Cream polyester felt, Hobbycraft

FALLEN FOR A PRICEY WALLPAPER? INSTEAD OF USING ALL-OVER, CUT COSTS WITH A SINGLE PANEL BEHIND THE BED FOR A LUXE HIT OF PATTERN

Mosslanda 55cm picture ledges, Ikea

8 GO FOR A SLIMLINE SHELF

Use a couple of Ikea picture ledges and make a super-clever bedside shelf. A brilliant idea in a small bedroom, it requires two of the smaller-sized ledges – and at £5 each, will cost just £10 to put together. Start by fixing the first ledge in position, right side up, on the wall next to the bed. Then turn your second ledge upside down and fix in place directly on top of the first shelf. It'll create a slimline surface for resting bedside bits and bobs.

9 Make easy under-bed storage

Find a new use for an old chest of drawers by recycling the individual drawers to make colourful under-bed storage. Start by measuring the height space under the bed to check the drawers will fit. Remove the original handles and give the drawers a light sanding and quick wipe down before painting. Spray paint the drawers the same colour, or for a fun look, try a mix of bright shades. Once painted, add new handles and a set of castors on each, so that they can be wheeled in and out easily.

Alex castors, Ikea

STAND A WOODEN CRATE ON ONE END TO MAKE A RUSTIC BEDSIDE TABLE. PAINT THE INSIDE OR LINE WITH PATTERNED WALLPAPER

Rio bed, Furniture and Choice

10 BRIGHTEN UP YOUR BEDROOM

Plain walls crying out for some colour? Have fun with a bold colour block look that will add instant impact for the cost of just a couple of pots of paint. Rather than re-doing the whole room, concentrate on the wall behind the bed to create a feature area that will become the room's focal point. Try a half-painted wall going diagonally, rather than horizontally, for a quirky effect. Fix decorator's tape from the top corner of the wall to the floor, to create a crisp diagonal dividing line between colours. Add mini polka dots or a circle feature on either side to add extra wow.

11 REVAMP PLAIN DRAWERS

Give a standard white chest of drawers an upgrade using wallpaper to transform the drawer fronts. Choose a small-scale pattern that's easily lined up or an assortment of designs to create a patchwork effect. Cut wallpaper to fit flush to the edges of each drawer front and stick into place using wallpaper paste or grab adhesive. Add new drawer pulls to complete the look.

For similar fabric, try Byron, Dunelm

Mix large and small-scale wallpapers in tonal colours

12 *Upgrade your headboard*

If you have an upholstered headboard that has seen better days, instead of replacing it entirely, try a quick 'no-sew' revamp and cover it with new fabric. An easy option for a standard headboard (one that doesn't have any fiddly buttoned upholstery), you'll need a length of fabric that measures the width and height of your headboard, plus an extra 20cm or so all round. Position your fabric centrally on the headboard, wrap the corners (like you would wrap a present) and staple at the back to secure. Hold the fabric taut as you work around, stapling the top edge first and then the sides. Ask someone to hold the fabric in place as you go.

FEATURE LISA FAZZANI PHOTOGRAPHS FUTURECONTENTHUB.COM

The New Look
MODERN VINTAGE

Take a relaxed vintage scheme up a level, by working in warm woods, luxe metallics and rich accent details

2. Add playful details

Scalloped edging on floating shelves gives a nostalgic, feminine feel, and can be painted to tie in with the rest of the decor. Style shelves with coloured glass, ceramics and luxe accessories.

1. Choose classic yet contemporary

Pick 1950s-style furniture that feels modern, with clean lines in honey-tone woods. A curvy dressing table with tapered legs is a must, teamed with a chest finished with glam marble-look tops and brass fittings.

FEATURE LAURA HIGGINS

3. Create wow-factor walls

Adding panelling to the lower third of a wall is a simple way to add character. Hang patterned wallpaper above, picking a bright shade from the design to paint the panelling and woodwork around the room.

MIRROR MIRROR
Dressing table mirror, Amazon Basics

SUNSET HUES
Glaze vase, Sass & Belle

FLORAL HIT
Flora quilted blanket, JYSK

Nail the style
DREAMY DECOR
Combine soft pastels and rusty tones

PILLOW TALK
CM Polycotton pair of pillowcases in rust, Habitat

4. Mix pastels with neutrals

Soft pinks and blues give a vintage feel, but adding warm neutrals will stop the scheme looking too saccharine. Opt for light linen-coloured bedding and a woven rug, plus hints of burnt orange for depth.

Design, Claire Kennedy @ck_homestyle for Dwell. Dormire double ottoman bed; Lineas rug; Molveno chest of drawers; Domina dressing table; Duo footstool; Terra vase; Perta table lamp; Libro bookends; Urto candle holder, all Dwell.

PLUSH POUFFE
Footstool, Homescapes

CANDLE LIGHT
Glass candle holder, Matalan

UNDER £200

TACTILE TOUCH
Pedersborg rug, Ikea

WALL DECOR
'I picked out the pink and green tones for both of the prints from Fy!'

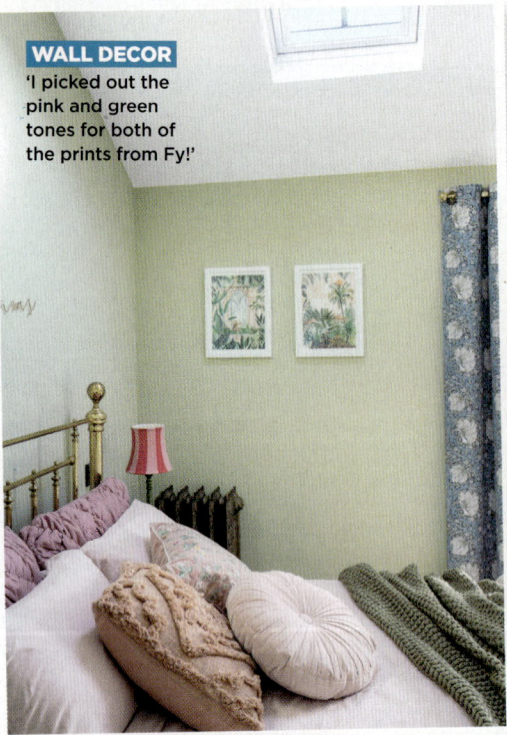

IDEA TO STEAL
'The brass bed frame and vintage-look radiator suit our period cottage'

sweet dreams

COME ON IN!

ABOUT ME I'm Sandra Knipe and I live with my husband Karl and cat Lucas in a three-bedroom period cottage in Enfield. We moved here in 2019.

THE CHALLENGE We had a garage that we just used for storage, but then in June 2021 we decided to extend and convert it into an additional bedroom, complete with a dressing area and a bathroom.

MY WISH LIST I wanted the new space to have high ceilings, because the rest of the house is a low-beamed cottage. We also decided to include an en-suite bathroom off the new bedroom and give it access to the garden with double doors.

SOOTHING PALETTE
'Farrow & Ball's Cooking Apple Green inspired the colour scheme in the bedroom and I've paired it with pink touches for a feminine vibe'

of OLD AND NEW'

A new extension gave Sandra Knipe the chance to flex her creative skills and design a brand new luxurious bedroom suite

I've always been drawn to period properties and when my husband Karl and I saw our 1650s cottage in Enfield it was love at first sight,' says Sandra. 'The place was in good condition, but it had been decorated in a very modern way, which didn't suit the style of the house. Bit by bit we began changing it to a more traditional look, with lots of vintage buys combined with heritage colours and prints. We took our time and finally had it looking just how we wanted it.

Then, in 2021, we made the decision to extend the house to include a third bedroom, which would not only give us a larger sleep space, but also a dressing area and en-suite bathroom.

Planning starts

We had a garage at the side of the house, and decided to use this as part of the extra bedroom space. We hired builders to brick up the garage doors and fit new windows, along with an internal door and walkway into the rest of the house.

I knew I wanted the new extension to feel spacious, so we asked for high ceilings, and as the bedroom would back onto the garden, which overlooks the countryside, we decided to have French doors to make the most of the view.

Looking at the layout

Building began and over the next three months the extension was built and plastered, with wooden floorboards fitted over a new insulated floor, which we sanded and oiled. Our build costs did go up quite a lot over these months, as it was during lockdown and materials like paint, wood and tools were a hot commodity.

Once the overall structure was built, we did a walk round with the builders to work out where to put the internal ▶▶

TOTAL £8,997

TURN OVER FOR MY SHOPPING LIST

walls, as the space would be split into three (for the bedroom, en suite and dressing room). Because the height of the extension was a decent size, we were also able to include an open loft area, which we use as a snug. It's one of the features that makes this space feel so unique.

Smart storage

Adding bespoke wardrobes to the dressing area was key and we chose Elle wardrobes in Clover from My Fitted Bedroom, which have a traditional look with their panelled design. When the team visited to measure up, they gave us some good tips on how to maximise the space. Once we were happy with the design, they were fitted within two days. We couldn't be happier with them; we've got more wardrobe space than we've ever had before and even managed to fit in a dressing table, too.

We both like a mix of old and new and wanted the bedroom to have some quirky touches. We had some wood left over from the build, so I looked online and found some mouldings to decorate it. We hung it above the blind and it's a unique touch that gives the space personality. We also bought a vintage leather suitcase from Camden market and an old Ercol-style chair on eBay for just £20. We also bought some old light switches from an antiques fair, but the electrician got an electric shock while fitting them, so we had to buy new ones!

Bedroom goals

In the main bedroom area, we went with a pretty pink and green scheme, painting the walls in Cooking Apple Green by Farrow & Ball. I chose curtains with a William Morris print, while the rattan bedside tables and a bamboo chair and ceiling light from Dunelm give the space a relaxed look. Our bed and the bedding were bargain buys in the sales, and I added some throws and cushions in pink and green shades to complete the scheme. We're so happy with how it's turned out and the view out to the garden is just beautiful.

'I LOVE ANTIQUES SHOPS FOR ONE-OFF BUYS. YOU NEVER KNOW WHAT YOU MIGHT DISCOVER AND COME HOME WITH'

OPEN UP
'The dressing area is open to our bedroom – we chose not to have a door so made sure the decor tied in'

Make it!
DECORATIVE MOULDING

✳ Take a piece of wood and sand the surface and edges to make sure it's smooth, while at the same time providing a key for the mouldings to stick to.

✳ Source some mouldings and use wood glue to attach them to the piece of wood. Sandra found her chosen mouldings at baileasinteriors.co.uk.

✳ Paint the mouldings and wood panel in the same colour as the rest of the woodwork to create a decorative panel that gives the period feel you're looking for.

Where to buy Sandra's style

Walls painted in Cooking Apple Green emulsion, Farrow & Ball. Woodwork in Putti intelligent eggshell, Little Greene. Bed, Feather & Black. Indi bedside tables; Miah rattan pendant light; scalloped tray; chunky knit throw in Olive; 'Sweet Dreams' metal wire words, all Dunelm. The Josie Rattan flower chair, from Roseland, is similar. Shaker Continental wardrobes in Clover, My Fitted Bedroom. Paladin Oxford cast-iron radiators, Trade Radiators. William Morris Pimpernel blush curtains, Curtains2Go. Art Nouveau Dolly light switches, Broughtons. Gallery Home Sullana rug, Next, is similar to this. Try Ruby duvet cover set in Powder Pink, Sazy. Jungle Swing art print; Victorian Greenhouse art print, both Fy! Shaggy cushion in Old Rose, Spicer & Wood.

IDEA TO STEAL

'We added a brass rail to the outside of our wardrobes so we can hang our outfits for next day'

CLEVER STORAGE

'We had an extra wardrobe fitted in our bedroom which also houses a TV'

MAKE-UP STATION

'My Fitted Bedroom helped us create lots of storage in this space and even built in a dressing table to match the wardrobes'

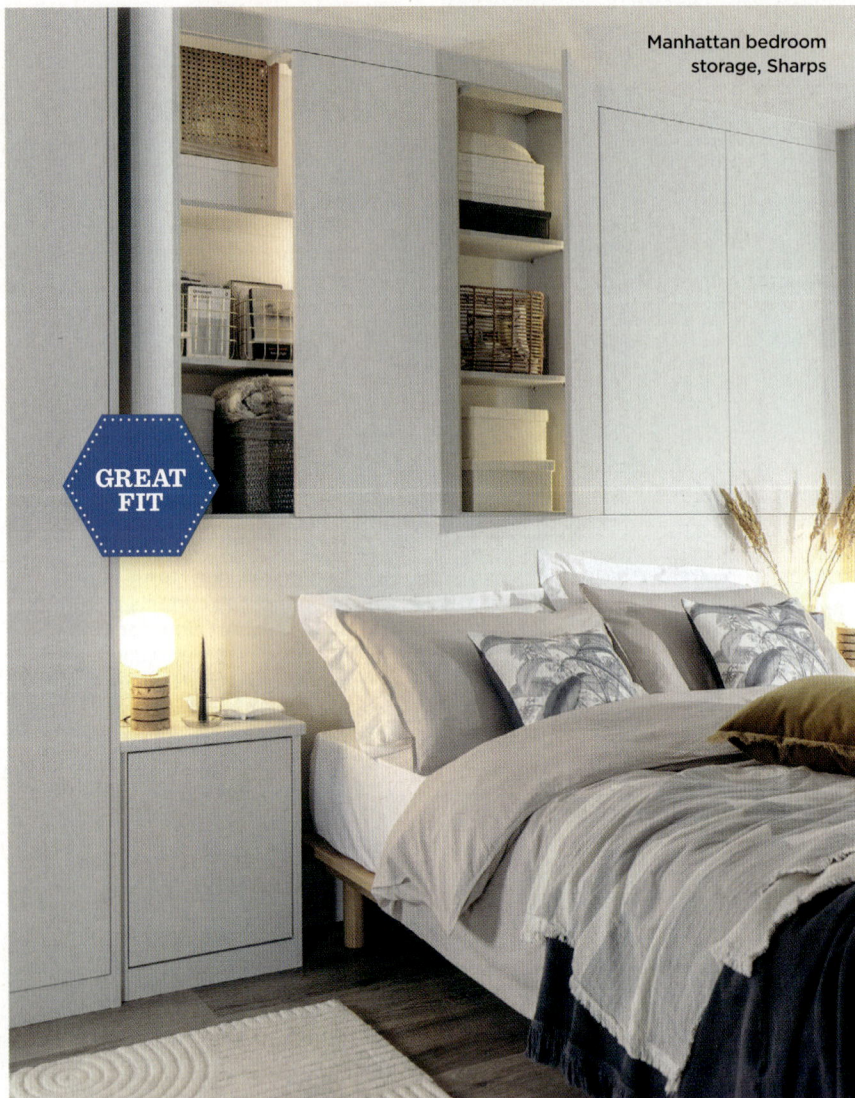

Manhattan bedroom storage, Sharps

GREAT FIT

Utilise wasted wall space behind a bed with a bank of overhead units spanning the gap between two wardrobes. Bridge units can be tailored to incorporate bedside cabinets, cubbies and shelving for stowing clothes, bedding and other bedside essentials.

Bekvam spice racks, Ikea

FIX RACKS TO A WALL

Tame untidy toiletries and hair-styling essentials by creating a mini styling station beside a dressing table. This smart storage hack uses a trio of wooden spice racks fixed to the wall for holding bottles, tubs and tubes. The bottom rack has been attached upside-down with S-hooks on the rail so a hairdryer, comb and towels can be handily hung.

Bedroom
STORAGE

Find space you didn't know you had, with hidden storage and neat space-saving hacks

Hemnes shoe cabinet, Ikea

When it comes to bedroom furniture, the combination of bed, wardrobe, chest of drawers and bedside table seems to be the standard set-up for many of us. And while these pieces offer an adequate amount of storage, it often turns out to be just not quite enough.

Finding ways to incorporate extra storage into a bedroom can be a challenge, especially if it's a small or average-sized space. But working in storage around, under and above existing furniture can be a savvy way of squeezing in more without making the room feel cramped or overcrowded – and it needn't break the bank.

GOING UP

Square raffia baskets, Vibrant Home

ADD A SHELF UP HIGH

Make use of the height in a small box bedroom by slotting in a wide shelf just below ceiling level. This is ideal for stacking bedtime reading material – or add a line-up of sturdy grab-handle baskets so that bits and bobs can be kept out of sight for a neat, organised look.

Trones shoe cabinet, Ikea

TRY HIDEAWAY STORAGE

The best storage ideas are the ones you don't spot right away. This 'secret' storage headboard is made of slimline shoe cubbies attached to the wall. It provides a narrow shelf for a decorative display, while the drop-down drawers are perfect for spare bedlinen, pyjamas or books.

Havsta two-door cabinets, Ikea

'USE WASTED SPACE UNDER BEDS TO STOW OUT-OF-SEASON CLOTHES IN LIDDED DRAWERS TO PROTECT THEM FROM DUST'

LISA FAZZANI, EDITOR

SLOT IN A VANITY UNIT

Think you can't squeeze in a make-up station? Think again. This clever hack repurposes a slimline shoe cabinet that's only 22cm deep, so can be slotted into an alcove without taking up tons of floor space. With drop-down cubbies it requires less opening space than drawers and has only front legs so it can butt up neatly against a wall.

CREATE A HANDY BED-END BANK

Boost storage with a row of low cabinets positioned at the end of the bed – great for bulky bedding and blankets or in a study-bedroom for books and paperwork. Make sure the cabinets roughly match the width of the bed, even if you have to put a couple side by side, and paint in the same shade as the headboard for a unified look.

FEATURE LISA FAZZANI, JENNIFER EBERT PHOTOGRAPHS FUTURECONTENTHUB.COM